THIS BOOK BELONGS TO

The Library of

....

....

I can't tell you how grateful I am that you decided to read my book. My most heartfelt thanks that you took time out of your life to choose my work and I hope you find benefit within these pages.

There are so many books available today that offer similar content so that makes it even more humbling that you decided to buying mine.

Tell me what you thought! I am eager to hear your opinion and ideas on what you read as are others who are looking for a good book to buy. Leave a review on Amazon.com so others can benefit from your wisdom!

With much thanks.

Table of Contents

SUMMARY

The rise of e-commerce, particularly the dominance of Amazon, has revolutionized the way people shop and conduct business. With the advent of the internet and technological advancements, online shopping has become increasingly popular and convenient for consumers worldwide.

Amazon, founded by Jeff Bezos in 1994, started as an online bookstore but quickly expanded its product offerings to include a wide range of items. Today, it is the largest online retailer in the world, offering millions of products across various categories such as electronics, clothing, home goods, and more. Its success can be attributed to its customer-centric approach, competitive pricing, and efficient delivery system.

One of the key factors that contributed to the rise of e-commerce and Amazon is the convenience it offers to consumers. With just a few clicks, shoppers can browse through a vast selection of products, compare prices, read reviews, and make purchases from the comfort of their own homes. This eliminates the need to physically visit multiple stores, saving time and effort. Additionally, e-commerce allows consumers to shop at any time of the day, making it particularly appealing for those with busy schedules or limited access to physical stores.

Another significant advantage of e-commerce is the ability to reach a global audience. Unlike traditional brick-and-mortar stores, online retailers like Amazon can cater to customers from all over the world. This has opened up new opportunities for businesses to expand their reach and tap into previously untapped markets. Furthermore, e-commerce platforms provide a level playing field for small businesses and entrepreneurs, allowing them to compete with larger, established brands.

Amazon's success can also be attributed to its focus on customer satisfaction. The company has invested heavily in building a robust customer service infrastructure, ensuring that shoppers have a seamless experience from browsing to delivery. Its customer reviews and ratings system also helps build trust and confidence among consumers, enabling them to make informed purchasing decisions.

In addition to its e-commerce platform, Amazon has diversified its business by offering various services such as Amazon Prime, which provides subscribers with benefits like free two-day shipping, access to streaming services, and exclusive deals. This has further solidified its position as a leader in the industry and has contributed to its loyal customer base.

However, the rise of e-commerce and Amazon has not been without its challenges. Traditional brick-and-mortar retailers have faced increased competition and have had to adapt their business models to stay relevant.

Dropshipping is a business model in which an online retailer does not keep products in stock but instead transfers customer orders and shipment details to the manufacturer, another retailer, or a wholesaler, who then ships the products directly to the customer. In this model, the retailer acts as a middleman, facilitating the transaction between the customer and the supplier.

The process of dropshipping begins when a customer places an order on the retailer's website. The retailer then forwards the order and shipping details to the supplier, who is responsible for packaging and shipping the product directly to the customer. The retailer does not handle the physical product, eliminating the need for inventory management, warehousing, and fulfillment operations.

One of the key advantages of dropshipping is that it allows entrepreneurs to start an online business with minimal upfront investment. Since there is no need to purchase inventory in advance, entrepreneurs can focus on building their online store, marketing their products, and driving traffic to their website. This significantly reduces the financial risk associated with traditional retail models, where large amounts of capital are required to purchase and store inventory.

Another benefit of dropshipping is the flexibility it offers. Retailers can easily add or remove products from their online store without the need to physically handle the inventory. This allows them to quickly adapt to changing market trends and customer demands. Additionally, dropshipping enables retailers to offer a wide range of products without the need to invest in a large inventory. They can partner with multiple suppliers and offer a diverse selection of products to their customers.

Dropshipping also provides retailers with the opportunity to scale their business rapidly. Since they are not limited by inventory constraints, they can easily handle a high volume of orders without the need for additional storage space or staff. This scalability allows entrepreneurs to grow their business quickly and efficiently.

However, dropshipping does have its challenges. One of the main concerns is the lack of control over the fulfillment process. Since the retailer relies on the supplier to handle packaging and shipping, there is a risk of delays, errors, or damaged products. This can negatively impact the customer experience and the retailer's reputation. It is crucial for retailers to carefully choose reliable suppliers and establish clear communication channels to mitigate these risks.

Furthermore, dropshipping can be highly competitive, as it is a popular business model that attracts many entrepreneurs. Retailers need to differentiate themselves by offering unique products, excellent customer service, and effective marketing strategies.

Setting up your Amazon Seller Account is a crucial step in starting your journey as an online seller. It allows you to tap into the vast customer base of Amazon and showcase your products to millions of potential buyers. In this guide, we will walk you through the process of setting up your Amazon Seller Account, providing you with a comprehensive understanding of the steps involved.

To begin, you need to visit the Amazon Seller Central website and click on the Register Now button. This will take you to the registration page where you will be prompted to provide your basic information such as your name, email address, and phone number. It is important to ensure that the information you provide is accurate and up-to-date as this will be used for communication purposes throughout your selling journey.

Once you have entered your personal information, you will be asked to choose the type of seller account you want to create. Amazon offers two options: Individual and Professional. The Individual account is suitable for sellers who plan to sell fewer than 40 items per month, while the Professional account is designed for sellers who anticipate selling more than 40 items per month. Consider your selling goals and volume before making a decision.

After selecting the account type, you will be required to provide additional information such as your business name, address, and bank account details. It is important to note that Amazon requires sellers to have a valid bank account in order to receive payments for their sales. Make sure to provide accurate banking information to avoid any delays in receiving your funds.

Once you have completed the registration process, you will need to set up your seller profile. This includes creating a unique display name that will be visible to customers, as well as providing a brief description of your business and the products you plan to sell. It is crucial to create a compelling and informative seller profile as it helps build trust and credibility with potential buyers.

Next, you will need to configure your shipping settings. Amazon provides various shipping options, including fulfillment by Amazon (FBA) where Amazon handles the storage, packaging, and shipping of your products. Alternatively, you can choose to fulfill orders yourself, known as merchant-fulfilled. Carefully consider the pros and cons of each option and select the one that aligns with your business model and resources.

Once you have set up your shipping settings, you will need to list your products on Amazon. This involves providing detailed information about each product, including its title, description, images, and pricing.

Building a professional website involves several steps and considerations to ensure that the final product meets the desired objectives and effectively represents the brand or business. This process typically includes planning, design, development, and testing.

The first step in building a professional website is planning. This involves defining the goals and objectives of the website, identifying the target audience, and determining the key features and functionalities required. It is important to have a clear understanding of the purpose of the website and what it needs to achieve in order to guide the design and development process.

Once the planning phase is complete, the next step is design. This involves creating a visual representation of the website, including the layout, color scheme, typography, and overall aesthetic. The design should be aligned with the brand identity and reflect the desired image or message. It is important to create a user-friendly and intuitive design that enhances the user experience and encourages engagement.

After the design is finalized, the development phase begins. This involves translating the design into a functional website using coding languages such as HTML, CSS, and JavaScript. The development process includes creating the website structure, implementing the design elements, and integrating any necessary functionalities such as contact forms, e-commerce capabilities, or content management systems. It is important to ensure that the website is responsive and compatible with different devices and browsers to reach a wider audience.

Once the development is complete, the website needs to be thoroughly tested to ensure its functionality and performance. This includes checking for any bugs or errors, testing the website's responsiveness and compatibility, and conducting user testing to gather feedback and make necessary improvements. Testing is crucial to ensure that the website functions as intended and provides a seamless user experience.

In addition to the technical aspects, building a professional website also involves creating high-quality and engaging content. This includes well-written copy, compelling images or videos, and relevant information that effectively communicates the brand's message and engages the target audience. Content should be optimized for search engines to improve visibility and attract organic traffic.

Building a professional website is an ongoing process that requires regular updates and maintenance. It is important to regularly review and update the content, monitor website performance, and make necessary improvements to ensure that the website remains relevant, functional, and effective in achieving its goals.

Crafting compelling product titles and descriptions is a crucial aspect of marketing and selling products. The input task involves creating longer and more detailed content for this specific topic.

When it comes to product titles, it is essential to capture the attention of potential customers and convey the unique selling points of the product. A compelling title should be concise yet descriptive, providing a clear idea of what the product is and why it stands out from the competition. It should also incorporate relevant keywords to improve search engine optimization (SEO) and increase the chances of the product being discovered by online shoppers.

In addition to a captivating title, crafting compelling product descriptions is equally important. A well-written description can make a significant impact on a customer's decision-making process. It should provide detailed information about the product's features, benefits, and specifications. By highlighting the product's key attributes and explaining how it can solve a customer's problem or fulfill a need, a compelling description can effectively persuade potential buyers to make a purchase.

To create compelling product titles and descriptions, it is crucial to understand the target audience and their needs. Conducting market research and analyzing customer feedback can provide valuable insights into what customers are looking for and what language resonates with them. By tailoring the titles and descriptions to address the specific pain points and desires of the target audience, businesses can increase the chances of attracting and converting potential customers.

Furthermore, incorporating storytelling techniques into product descriptions can make them more engaging and memorable. By creating a narrative around the product, businesses can evoke emotions and connect with customers on a deeper level. This storytelling approach can help customers envision themselves using the product and experiencing the benefits it offers, ultimately increasing their desire to purchase.

In the digital age, where online shopping has become increasingly prevalent, optimizing product titles and descriptions for search engines is crucial. By conducting keyword research and incorporating relevant keywords into the content, businesses can improve their visibility in search engine results pages (SERPs). This, in turn, can drive more organic traffic to their product pages and increase the likelihood of conversions.

In conclusion, Amazon PPC Advertising is a powerful tool for sellers to promote their products on Amazon's platform. It offers targeted advertising, cost-effectiveness, and valuable data insights, allowing sellers to increase their visibility, attract potential customers, and optimize their advertising strategies. By leveraging the benefits of Amazon PPC Advertising, sellers can boost their sales and grow their business on the world's largest online marketplace.

Dealing with Suspensions and Policy Violations can be a challenging and sensitive task for any organization. It requires careful consideration of the circumstances surrounding the violation, as well as a fair and consistent approach to enforcing policies and disciplinary actions.

When an employee or member of an organization violates a policy, it is important to first gather all relevant information and evidence related to the incident. This may involve conducting interviews, reviewing documentation, or consulting with witnesses or other parties involved. It is crucial to ensure that the investigation is thorough and unbiased, as any inconsistencies or biases in the process can undermine the credibility of the disciplinary action.

Once all the necessary information has been gathered, it is important to review the organization's policies and guidelines to determine the appropriate course of action. This may involve consulting with legal counsel or human resources professionals to ensure that the chosen disciplinary action aligns with legal requirements and best practices.

In some cases, a suspension may be deemed necessary as a disciplinary measure. A suspension can range in duration depending on the severity of the violation and the organization's policies. During the suspension period, the employee or member is typically prohibited from participating in any work-related activities or accessing organizational resources. This serves as a temporary removal from their role or position, allowing time for reflection, investigation, or corrective actions to be taken.

When implementing a suspension, it is important to communicate the decision clearly and effectively to the individual involved. This includes providing them with a written notice outlining the reasons for the suspension, the duration, and any conditions or expectations for reinstatement. It is crucial to maintain confidentiality and privacy throughout this process, ensuring that only those directly involved or with a legitimate need to know are informed about the suspension.

During the suspension period, it is important to regularly communicate with the individual to provide updates on the progress of the investigation or any additional actions being taken. This helps to maintain transparency and ensures that the individual is aware of the steps being taken to address the violation.

After the suspension period has ended, a thorough review of the incident and the individual's conduct should be conducted. This may involve further discussions, interviews, or assessments to determine the appropriate next steps. Depending on the outcome of this review, the individual may be reinstated, subject to additional disciplinary actions, or in some cases, terminated from their position or membership.

In this article, we will delve into a series of interviews conducted with successful Amazon dropshippers. These individuals have managed to build thriving businesses by leveraging the power of the Amazon platform and implementing effective dropshipping strategies.

The first interviewee, John, shared his journey of becoming a successful Amazon dropshipper. He emphasized the importance of thorough market research and finding profitable niches with high demand and low competition. John explained that he spends a significant amount of time analyzing product trends, customer reviews, and competitor strategies to identify the most lucrative opportunities.

John also highlighted the significance of building strong relationships with reliable suppliers. He emphasized the need to find suppliers who can consistently provide high-quality products at competitive prices. According to John, maintaining open lines of communication with suppliers is crucial for ensuring smooth operations and timely order fulfillment.

Another interviewee, Sarah, emphasized the importance of optimizing product listings on Amazon. She stressed the significance of using relevant keywords, compelling product descriptions, and high-quality images to attract potential customers. Sarah also highlighted the importance of obtaining positive customer reviews, as they play a vital role in building trust and credibility for her business.

Both John and Sarah emphasized the importance of effective inventory management. They stressed the need to closely monitor stock levels, anticipate demand fluctuations, and ensure timely reordering to avoid stockouts. They also highlighted the importance of utilizing Amazon's FBA (Fulfillment by Amazon) service to streamline order fulfillment and enhance customer satisfaction.

In terms of marketing strategies, the interviewed dropshippers shared various approaches. John emphasized the power of social media advertising, particularly Facebook ads, to drive targeted traffic to his Amazon listings. He highlighted the importance of creating compelling ad copy and targeting specific demographics to maximize conversions.

Sarah, on the other hand, emphasized the significance of influencer marketing. She explained how she collaborates with relevant influencers in her niche to promote her products and reach a wider audience. Sarah also highlighted the importance of leveraging email marketing to nurture customer relationships and drive repeat purchases.

Both dropshippers acknowledged the challenges they faced along their journey. They emphasized the need for perseverance, adaptability, and continuous learning. They stressed the importance of staying updated with Amazon's policies and guidelines, as well as industry trends and best practices.

Staying compliant with Amazon policies is crucial for sellers who want to maintain a successful and sustainable business on the platform. Amazon has a set of strict guidelines and policies in place to ensure a positive customer experience and fair competition among sellers. Failing to adhere to these policies can result in penalties, account suspension, or even permanent removal from the platform.

One of the key policies that sellers need to be aware of is the product listing policy. Amazon requires sellers to provide accurate and detailed information about their products, including titles, descriptions, images, and categorization. Sellers must ensure that their listings are free from any misleading or false information. This includes avoiding exaggerated claims, using accurate product images, and providing clear and concise descriptions.

Another important policy is the customer review policy. Amazon places a high value on customer feedback and reviews, as they play a significant role in influencing purchasing decisions. Sellers are not allowed to manipulate or incentivize customers to leave positive reviews. This means that sellers should not offer discounts, free products, or any other form of compensation in exchange for reviews. Additionally, sellers should not engage in any activities that may artificially inflate their review ratings, such as creating multiple accounts to leave positive reviews.

Sellers also need to be aware of the policy regarding prohibited products. Amazon has a list of restricted and prohibited items that sellers are not allowed to sell on the platform. These include items such as counterfeit goods, illegal drugs, weapons, and hazardous materials. Sellers should thoroughly review this list and ensure that their products comply with all applicable laws and regulations.

Furthermore, sellers must comply with Amazon's policy on intellectual property rights. This means that sellers should not infringe on any copyrights, trademarks, or patents when creating their product listings. Sellers should also be cautious when using product images or descriptions that may be copyrighted by others.

In addition to these policies, sellers should also be aware of Amazon's policy on pricing and promotions. Amazon prohibits sellers from engaging in price gouging or artificially inflating prices. Sellers should also ensure that any promotions or discounts they offer are transparent and comply with Amazon's guidelines.

To stay compliant with Amazon policies, sellers should regularly review and familiarize themselves with the platform's policies and guidelines. It is also recommended to stay updated on any policy changes or updates that Amazon may announce. Sellers should also monitor their account performance and customer feedback to identify and address any potential policy violations.

Over the past few decades, the world of commerce has undergone a significant transformation with the rise of e-commerce and the emergence of dropshipping as a popular business model. This evolution has revolutionized the way people buy and sell products, creating new opportunities for entrepreneurs and consumers alike.

E-commerce, or electronic commerce, refers to the buying and selling of goods and services over the internet. It has become increasingly popular due to its convenience and accessibility. With just a few clicks, consumers can browse through a wide range of products, compare prices, and make purchases from the comfort of their own homes. This shift towards online shopping has been driven by advancements in technology, such as the widespread availability of high-speed internet and the proliferation of smartphones.

One of the key factors that has contributed to the growth of e-commerce is the development of secure online payment systems. In the early days of online shopping, many consumers were hesitant to provide their credit card information online due to concerns about security. However, the introduction of encryption technology and the establishment of trusted payment gateways have helped to alleviate these concerns, making online transactions more secure and reliable.

Another significant development in the world of e-commerce is the rise of dropshipping. Dropshipping is a business model where the retailer does not keep the products in stock but instead transfers the customer orders and shipment details to the manufacturer, another retailer, or a wholesaler, who then ships the products directly to the customer. This eliminates the need for the retailer to invest in inventory and allows them to focus on marketing and customer service.

Dropshipping has gained popularity among entrepreneurs due to its low startup costs and flexibility. With traditional retail models, entrepreneurs would need to invest a significant amount of capital in purchasing inventory and setting up a physical store. However, with dropshipping, entrepreneurs can start their businesses with minimal upfront costs, as they only need to pay for the products once they have been sold. This makes it an attractive option for individuals looking to start their own online businesses.

Furthermore, dropshipping has also opened up opportunities for individuals to become online retailers without the need for specialized skills or expertise. With the advent of e-commerce platforms and marketplaces, such as Shopify and Amazon, entrepreneurs can easily set up their online stores and start selling products without the need for technical knowledge or web development skills. This has democratized the world of retail, allowing anyone with an internet connection and a passion for entrepreneurship to start their own online business.

Aspiring Amazon Dropshippers, I want to take a moment to encourage and inspire you on your journey towards success. Embarking on the path of dropshipping can be both exciting and challenging, but with the right mindset and strategies, you can achieve your goals and create a thriving business on Amazon.

First and foremost, it's important to believe in yourself and your abilities. Building a successful dropshipping business requires dedication, perseverance, and a strong belief in your own potential. Trust that you have what it takes to overcome obstacles and turn your dreams into reality.

One of the key factors in dropshipping success is thorough market research. Take the time to identify profitable niches and products that have a high demand but low competition. This will give you a competitive edge and increase your chances of success. Utilize tools and resources available to you, such as Amazon's own data and analytics, to make informed decisions about the products you choose to sell.

Another crucial aspect of dropshipping is building strong relationships with suppliers. Take the time to research and vet potential suppliers, ensuring they are reliable, trustworthy, and able to meet your customers' expectations. Communication is key in maintaining a healthy supplier relationship, so be proactive in reaching out and addressing any concerns or issues that may arise.

In addition to supplier relationships, customer satisfaction should be at the forefront of your business. Providing exceptional customer service and ensuring a seamless buying experience will not only lead to positive reviews and repeat customers but also help you stand out in a competitive marketplace. Respond promptly to customer inquiries, address any issues or concerns, and go above and beyond to exceed their expectations.

As you navigate the world of Amazon dropshipping, it's important to stay up to date with the latest trends and changes in the industry. Amazon is constantly evolving, and being aware of new policies, algorithms, and strategies will give you a competitive advantage. Join online communities, attend webinars, and read industry blogs to stay informed and continuously improve your business.

Lastly, don't be afraid to take risks and think outside the box. Dropshipping is a dynamic and ever-changing industry, and those who are willing to adapt and innovate are the ones who will thrive. Experiment with different marketing strategies, explore new product categories, and embrace new technologies to stay ahead of the curve.

Introduction

I'm going to show you a step by step plan on how you can make money by selling products on Amazon and other platforms via AMAZON PRIVATE LABELING. There's probably a million more ways to do it but I believe that if you follow the system that I will lay out to you, then you will make money.

As much as I wanted to guarantee that you will make a million dollars, I won't. Every business out there requires effort, a bit of investment and a lot of hard work to succeed. If you're in the PRIVATE LABELING business to get rich quick, then I'm sorry to tell you but this is not a get rich quick. However, if you're willing to take a few hours a day to work on your business, then you'll have a higher chance of succeeding.

Also, I wrote this book with the hope that it'll help guys like you quit their full time job. If you already quitted and you're already making an income online, well congratulations! If not, this book has the potential to help you do it.

What can you expect in this book?

Expect this book to be 90% actionable content. Most books out there about FBA are full of theories! They just want to get longer pages so they can sell their books at higher prices.

I'll be honest with you, I have no idea if this book will be 30 pages, 60 pages or 160.

What I know is I'm going to put everything that you need to at the very least get started in this business and have a good plan of attack for your business.

I hope that I can achieve that in this book.

Who shouldn't read this book?

If you are an information collector, please, stop reading, this book is not for you. If you are afraid of taking a bit of risk and afraid of failure, stop reading also, this book is not for you.

However, if you are ready to read and implement, continue reading because this book is for you.

For you to understand the whole process much better, in the next chapter I'm going to give you a sort of 1,000ft overview of the system.

You're going to learn what to do first, second, third and on and on.

Ready? Let's do this.

Here are 3 reasons why I would rather private label a product than to buy and sell different items online.

1 – Scalable
Unlike arbitrage buying (low) and selling (high) different products – you're not at the mercy of the original product seller. What if the store run out of that product? Then you're toast!

2 – Sustainable
Since you are building a brand, you are more likely to stay in the business.

3 – Million Dollar Exits
No branding means no company sale. If you are doing arbitrage, dropshipping and other methods, it is unlikely that others will want to buy your company since they can easily find the same product you are selling. If you have a private label business, it is less about the product than it is about the brand.

In the next page, I'll show you the exact step by step blueprint to making money via selling private label items on Amazon.

Step by Step

Here is the exact blueprint that you can follow in order to make a full time income via Amazon Private Labeling.

1 – Seller Account Creation
First step is definitely the easiest; you just have to create a seller central account.

2 – Product Ideas
The 2nd step is to know what makes a great product great, so you don't have to waste a lot of time and money evaluating products. Think of this as the pre-evaluation part.

3 – Product Evaluation
The next step is to find products that will sell constantly.

4 – Product Sourcing
Step # 4 is to find suppliers for your chosen product.

5 – Product Listing Formula
Then the last step is to create product listing that will rank higher in Amazon's search engine and most especially create a product listing that will convert into sales.
So that's the whole blueprint, without further ado, let's get started!

6 – Facebook Advertising

You'll also learn some basics about Facebook Advertising.
This technique will require you to have at least $10 per day in marketing budget. It'll be worth it though, since there's a growing amount of consumers directly buying from Facebook nowadays.

Chapter 1 - Finding a Profitable Product

Before we start researching a product idea, we have to know first what in the world are we looking for. We have to know what makes a great product great.

Here are the things that I look for when I'm doing my product research.

1   - Amazon allowed category

I always check if that type of product is in the Amazon allowed category. Most e-commerce businessman starts with Amazon as their launching pad. You might as well find something that you are allowed to sell there.

2   – 4x, 5x Rule

The price of the product should be 4x or 5x the amount it cost you to manufacture (outsource) per unit.

So if a product is selling on Amazon for $30, then your cost per unit shouldn't be more than $7. There are a lot of added cost for doing business such as shipping, packaging, labeling, marketing, Amazon fees etc. All of that could possible total to an additional $13 per unit. If you sell your product for $30 less $20 for overall expenses, this allows you a profit margin of 33% or $10. Not bad.

3   – Minimum Sales Price is $10 , or $20 for those who want to make more money ☺

I usually avoid a product that sells for less than $10. It's quite hard to make a good profit for a $10 product. I would rather put the same energy, time , money and effort in finding something that will make me a bigger profit margin.

4   – Light, relatively small and easy to ship

This is true especially if you are just starting out in the business. You have no idea how much shipping would eat up your profits specifically for products that are huge and heavy. Trust me, leave those products first and start with something light and easy to ship. However, if you insist, make sure first that the numbers makes sense. A good profit margin (NET) for me is at around 30% and above.

5   – Can be private labeled

This may vary depending on your preference. But if you truly want to build a real business with a brand name that you can be proud of. Then I would choose something that can be private labeled. Also, having a brand allows you to sell your company in the future for a 7 or 8 figure exit.

6 – Best Seller Ranking of less than 1,000 on Amazon (per category) (take note that Amazon have a lot of sub-categories) – Amazon Best Seller Ranking or BSR can be found on the product listing page.

Here's an example:

Let's say you wanted to sell a product on the bbq gloves niche.

If you type bbq gloves on Amazon's search product, you'll see the top 3 products. Open them and look at their BSR.

I would like to see the first product on the top 1-1000

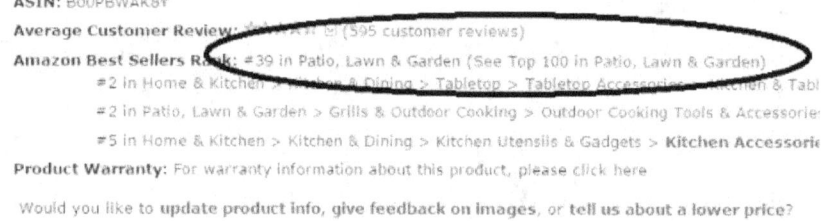

And the second product and third product on the listing to be at the top 1 – 3000

Item model number: MK-3988

Average Customer Review: ☆☆☆☆☆ (271 customer reviews)

Amazon Best Sellers Rank: #683 in Patio, Lawn & Garden (See Top 100 in Patio, Lawn & Garden)

　　#1 in Home Improvement > Safety & Security > Personal Protective Equipment > Hand & Arm

　　#6 in Patio, Lawn & Garden > Grills & Outdoor Cooking > Outdoor Cooking Tools & Accessories

Product Warranty: For warranty information about this product, please click here

Would you like to give feedback on images or tell us about a lower price?

7 – It's not a "me too" product

One of the best examples I can give you is that product itself, the bbq gloves. If you look at our metrics, the bbq gloves can be a very good opportunity. But hold your horses first, this product is a "me too" product.

If you look at the search results, you'll notice that there are over 4,248 products that pretty much sell the same thing.

1-16 of 4,248 results for "bbq gloves"

What's even worse is that their basically all the same product when it comes to their positioning in the market.

Look at the pictures, the way those products are sold. It's basically product after product of the same type.

Now, I'm not saying that you will not make money on this niche. If you are really good at marketing and you feel like you can outrank these products on the first page of Amazon search results, then by all means, go with these types of products. Also, if you can find a very good Unique Selling Proposition then this could be a very good opportunity for you.

Another important thing to consider is the way other e-commerce found this product. At the beginning of this book I told you about how most courses teach students to just look at the top 100 of Amazon. Well, those are your competition and most of them will be suckered into thinking that since this product is a top 100, then this must be a good product to sell. WRONG! There are already hundreds of people looking at this product; do you want to sell the same thing the other hundreds are already selling? Hmmm. Probably not.

8 – Evergreen Products

I usually avoid products that sells on a seasonal basis. I have no plan of making $10,000 on December and then $1,000 on January.

9 – Consumable*

This one is a bit optional. But it does makes sense to sell a consumable product since you'll get more repeat buyers instead of a sort of "one deal" products.

10 – I will use the product myself*

Just like #9, this one is optional. But for long term considerations, it would be nice to sell something you actually use and you really believe in. Plus it'll be much enjoyable to work.

11 – Number of reviews on Amazon for the top 3 products for the main keyword should be at the maximum of 300 for top 1 product, and 200 for the top 2 and 3 products.

If the top 3 has over 300+ reviews, I usually stay out of that market. (Especially if you are a beginner), But if you have some experience and you know you can beat them, then go on with that market.

If you are good at marketing (or if you are willing to study marketing), the number of reviews doesn't really matter that much.

The number of reviews just means that there are a lot of buyers in that market. Remember, competition is good!

12   – Merchant Words (Merchantwords.com)

I like to see my main keyword getting at least 10,000 searches on Merchantwords. It's basically a tool that gathers information from Amazon and other search engines, it's not accurate but it's close.

It's $30 per month but I'm pretty sure you can find a coupon for $9 a month. Just type "merchant words $9" on Google.

All right, I just saved you $21 per month; you might as well buy my next book about finding and negotiating with suppliers. It's not written yet, but it'll be up for sale soon for sure.

OKAY, sorry for my little advertisement there; let's just go straight to the next chapter, which is all about, organizing your product research.

13   – Is there room for improvement

If the products that are being sold kind of sucks then this could be a very good opportunity for you! You can create a better product, better market positioning and everything else.

If there is a room for improvement in that market, then that would be perfect for you.

This one takes a little bit of time and experience to understand. For now, try to understand the market wants and needs, read the reviews, most specially the negative reviews. It'll give you a lot of information about what the market wants and hates when it comes to that product.

Chapter 2 - Product Research & Evaluation

In this step, I'll teach you 3 of the best ways to find product opportunities. Also, I'll show you how you can evaluate if a product is more likely to make money or not.

1 - Supplier Reverse Engineering

Would you believe me if I told you that only 1 out of every 100 E-commerce owners use this method for their research? I hope so. Do I have proof? No I don't. But I 100% believe that to be true.

What I would do is I'll go to ALIBABA.COM, which is pretty much the largest source of supplier's list for different products.

Then I'll go to different categories and check different products available for manufacturing and private labeling.

:≡ CATEGORIES

Apparel, Textiles & Accessories	**Gifts & Crafts**	**Sports & Entertainment**
	Metal Crafts	Outdoor Sports
Auto & Transportation	Wood Crafts	Fitness & Body Building
Electronics	Crystal Crafts	Water Sports
	Paper Crafts	Amusement Parks
Machinery, Industrial Parts & Tools	Resin Crafts	Musical Instruments
	Plastic Crafts	Indoor Sports
Gifts, Sports & Toys	Glass Crafts	Team Sports
	Bamboo Crafts	Winter Sports
Home, Lights & Construction	Event & Party Supplies	View All Categories
Health & Beauty	Christmas Decoration Supplies	
	Painting & Calligraphy	**Toys & Hobbies**
Bags, Shoes & Accessories	Key Chains	
	Frame	Toy Vehicles & RC Toys
Electrical Equipment, Components & Telecom	Stickers	Outdoor Toys
	View All Categories	Inflatable Bouncers
Agriculture & Food		Educational Toys
Packaging, Advertising & Office		Action Figures
		Plush Toys
Metallurgy, Chemicals, Plastics		

I'll look at different product and just spend hours here looking for opportunities.

If you found an interesting product, do the usual drill which is to plug that product name in Amazon and see if it makes sense to add on our excel spreadsheet.

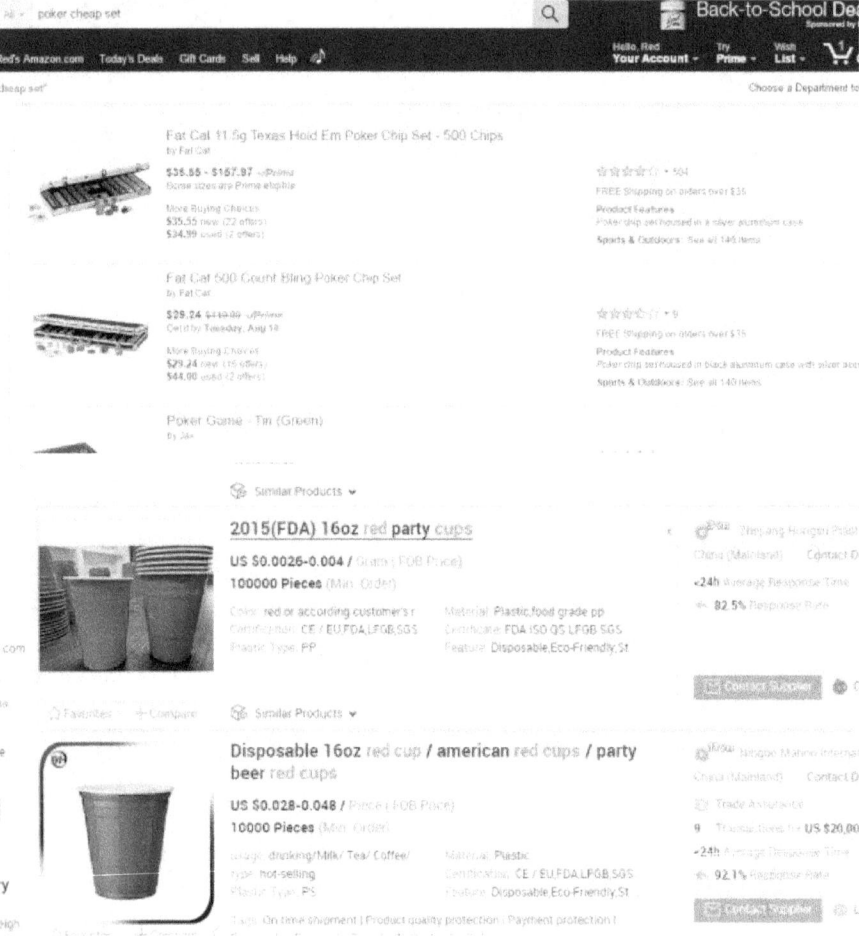

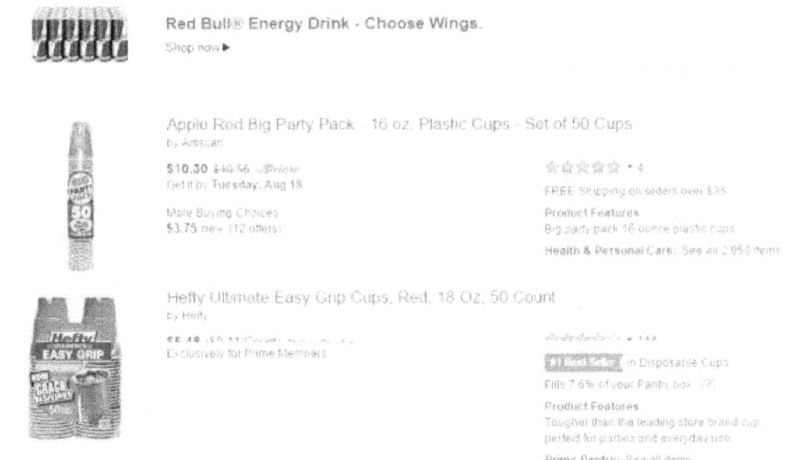

Red Bull® Energy Drink - Choose Wings.
Shop now ▶

Apple Red Big Party Pack - 16 oz. Plastic Cups - Set of 50 Cups
by Amscan

$10.30 $49.56 √Prime
Get it by Tuesday, Aug 18

More Buying Choices
$3.75 new (12 offers)

☆☆☆☆☆ • 4

FREE Shipping on orders over $35

Product Features
Big party pack 16 ounce plastic cups

Health & Personal Care: See all 2,950 items

Hefty Ultimate Easy Grip Cups, Red, 18 Oz, 50 Count
by Hefty

$5.48 ($0.11/Count)
Exclusively for Prime Members

☆☆☆☆☆ • 144

#1 Best Seller in Disposable Cups

Fills 7.6% of your Pantry box (?)

Product Features
Tougher than the leading store brand cup, perfect for parties and everyday use

Prime Pantry: See all items

6 – Amazon Top 100

Notice how this technique is not the first tactic that I recommend? I'm glad you did. Amazon's top 100 is great but you just can't solely rely on it for research.

To find the top 100, Go to Amazon.com and click on FULL STORE DIRECTORY.

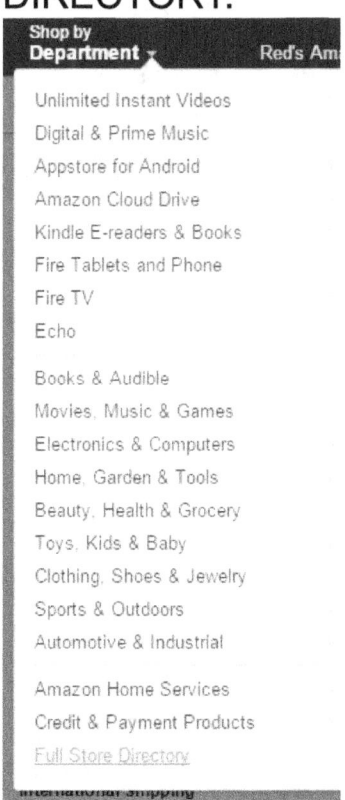

Shop by Department ▾   Red's Ama

Unlimited Instant Videos
Digital & Prime Music
Appstore for Android
Amazon Cloud Drive
Kindle E-readers & Books
Fire Tablets and Phone
Fire TV
Echo

Books & Audible
Movies, Music & Games
Electronics & Computers
Home, Garden & Tools
Beauty, Health & Grocery
Toys, Kids & Baby
Clothing, Shoes & Jewelry
Sports & Outdoors
Automotive & Industrial

Amazon Home Services
Credit & Payment Products
Full Store Directory

International Shipping

If you are a beginner, I suggest that you start with these 2 categories.

Home, Garden & Tools
Sports & Outdoors

Home, Garden & Tools

Home
Kitchen & Dining
Furniture & Décor
Bedding & Bath
Appliances
Patio, Lawn & Garden
Fine Art
Arts, Crafts & Sewing
Pet Supplies
Wedding Registry
Home Improvement
Power & Hand Tools
Lamps & Light Fixtures
Kitchen & Bath Fixtures
Hardware
Home Automation

Beauty, Health & Grocery

All Beauty
Luxury Beauty

Sports & Outdoors

Athletic Clothing
Exercise & Fitness
Hunting & Fishing
Team Sports
Fan Shop
Golf
Leisure Sports & Game Room
Sports Collectibles
All Sports & Fitness
Camping & Hiking
Cycling
Outdoor Clothing
Scooters, Skateboards & Skates
Water Sports
Winter Sports
Climbing
Accessories
All Outdoor Recreation

Automotive & Industrial

Click on bestsellers

Kitchen & Dining   Best Sellers

I would suggest that you look at the top 100 on different categories and find some products that seem to appear over and over again. If you found that, say a water pitcher appeared twice on the top 100 best seller list, it could be a good idea to dig deep on that

Repeat the process on different categories. Don't forget to look at their BSR, reviews and other factors I told you about on last few chapters.

7 – Amazon's top 100-500

This one is a little bit tricky because Amazon doesn't really have a top 100-500 best seller list.

What you can do is to check on top 100 SUB- CATEGORIES and click on some products and check their BSR manually.

Here's an example:

In the Kitchen & Dining category, I open the Bakeware sub-category and open some product listings inside.

I click on the silicone baking cups and look at its BSR.

Product Details

Shipping Weight: 4.8 ounces (View shipping rates and policies)

ASIN: B00N4ONBGY

Average Customer Review: ★★★★☆ (112 customer reviews)

Amazon Best Sellers Rank: #141 in Kitchen & Dining (See Top 100 in Kitchen & Dining)
    #1 in Kitchen & Dining > Bakeware > Baking Tools & Accessories > Baking Cups
    #37 in Kitchen & Dining > Kitchen Utensils & Gadgets

Would you like to give feedback on images or tell us about a lower price?

It's 141 in Kitchen and Dining.

If I just look at the category top 100, I never would have know that this product still have the attributes to be on my excel spreadsheet product list.

See more choices

The New York Baking
Company | 24-pack Reusable
Silicone Baking Cups /
Cupcake Liners
by The New York Baking Company

$9.24 $14.96 *Prime*
Get it by Tuesday, Aug 18
More Buying Choices
$7.98 new (11 offers)
FREE Shipping on orders over $35
☆☆☆☆☆ ▾ 1,216

[24 Pack] Ipow Silicone
Baking Cups Cupcake
Bakeware Liners Case Molds
Sets
by IPOW

$10.89 $29.99 *Prime*
Get it by Tuesday, Aug 18
FREE Shipping on orders over $35
#1 Best Seller in Baking Cups
☆☆☆☆☆ ▾ 112

Globally Good® Silicone
Baking Cups / Cupcake
Liners - 12 Reusable Muffin
Molds in Storage Container
by Globally Good

$7.99 $49.99 *Prime*
Get it by Tuesday, Aug 18
FREE Shipping on orders over $35
☆☆☆☆☆ ▾ 257

See more choices

Set of 12 Coloured Silicone
Cupcake / Muffin Cases 2.8"
by Kitchen Craft

$3.32
More Buying Choices
$2.31 new (12 offers)
FREE Shipping
☆☆☆☆☆ ▾ 411

This one seem like a "me too" product (it's already saturated with the same product and same positioning for that product) but if you can create a better USP and better marketing, then this could be a great product. Don't choose this product though just because I say so. Do your own research, I gave you everything you need to find a great product, use them.

For a second thought, I think this product sucks (importing wise), especially for beginners.

Remember, use the checklist I gave you when you're choosing a product to add in your list.

Evaluating your top 30

Once you have your top 30 list, it's time to evaluate and make it as small a list as possible.

I will make the evaluation process really easy for you.

You just have to answer the questions related to our preferences and you'll be on your way to choosing a profitable product.

The evaluation process will be broken down into 2 parts.

First evaluation and final evaluation.

For your first evaluation, you just have to answer YES and NO to the following questions.

1 – Does it have private label potential? (Answer should be YES)

2 – Can it be sold for at least $10? (Answer should be YES)

3 – Will it be expensive to ship? (Answer should be NO)

4 – Is it durable and not prone to breakage? (Answer should be YES)

5 – Is it in the Amazon allowed category? (Answer should be YES)

6 – Is there any potential to sell related items in that niche? (Answer should be YES)

7 – Is the sales price x4 or x5 your Cost of goods sold?? (refer to the 4x,5x rule) (Answer should be YES)

8 – Is the BSR for the top 1 product on the top 1 – 2,000 for that category. (Answer should be YES)

If the product miss one or two at max, then throw it away. Well don't throw it away, you might still use it in the future.

Once you got the answer for these questions and you have evaluated your product, you'll probably come up with a list of less than 10 or maybe even less than 5 if you really did the grunt work on the product research part. In fact, you probably don't even have to do this final evaluation if you already have a top 3.

Now, this is where the magic happens. This is where the rubber meets the road, where the pedal hits the metal, where Ronda Rousey knocks out Floyd Mayweather Jr. cold.

It's time to know the sales potential for all of these products.

Determine first the top 5 keywords use by your competition, What are the possible keywords that they are using so that customers in Amazon will see their product listing.

If it is a product about making pop molded ice cream, then the answers would be…

Pop molds

Ice cream molds

Pop mold silicone

Pop maker

Popsicle maker

Now, how can you come up with these keywords?

Well, you can use tools like keyword Google planner and merchant words.

Here are things to consider when you're trying to evaluate your top 3 products.

- Your 5 keywords should get at least 30,000 – 50,000 in total searches on Merchant words
- There's a variety of price points
- High BSR – 1-1000
- Reviews are quite low for top 2-5 products (means there is room for improvements)
- No more than 2 products with 300 plus review (again, this depends if you know marketing)
- Consistent average review for most listings – also means there are improvements that you can make for that product – that's a good opportunity)
- I will also look at "Google Trends" to see if this product/market is on the rise or if it is a bit outdated already.

Study your niche and the overall feel of your market. Then follow the guidelines I gave you above.

Once you got your top 3, it's on to the next step.

Chapter 3 – Finding a Supplier

Most people get stuck on this part, don't be most people! Understand that once you complete this part, then you are way ahead of the pack.
Here are 4 of the best ways to find suppliers. I recommend that you start with the first technique, then if you still can't find your preferred supplier, you can then try the other methods.

This is probably the most important chapter in this book. Why? because this is the part where most people give up! A lot of newbies have a hard time finding products that they can sell for a profit. I must admit, the beginnings will always be the hardest because you still have to get a feel of your market. But once you're *"battle tested"* and more experienced, you'll find this step much easier.

I'm going to teach you six ways to find products. These are the same methods that I use every day in finding great products. You don't have to do all of them at once (that would be crazy), you just have to pick one and focus on that for a few days or weeks till you find a good product that you want to target.

The product that you will choose will always depend on how much you want to earn. If you want to earn $10 sale then obviously, you can't choose a product priced at less than $30. I found that net profits (profit after advertisements, shipping, other fees etc) are usually at 30%-50% of the total sales revenue. Don't be afraid to start small though.

Method # 0 - The non-obvious - obvious method , also, a note on Private Labels and how to find them.

You will hate me for even including this in the book, but it has to be mention.

The first method is by doing a google search, I know... duhhh..
But I see a lot of newbies don't do this. I have no freakin idea why.

What you can do is to think of a product that you want to sell, say green juice powder. You simple type on Google " Green Juice Powder Manufacturer".

Another awesome search would be… "Green Juice Powder Suppliers" and my favorite… "Green Juice Powder *PRIVATE LABELS*"

The next thing that you should do is to compile a list of manufacturers and then email or call them. Not all will have what you need, or maybe the price is not right, whatever. Just continue to talk to manufacturers to also get a bit of experience on negotiating with suppliers.

On Private Labels...

Private labels are basically unbranded finished formula or product which you can brand as your own. You just have to choose the formulas and put your own brand and VOILA, you now have your own branded product.

Green Juice Powder private label

Web   Shopping   Images   News   Videos   More ▾   Search tools

About 204,000 results (0.43 seconds)

Private Label Supplement - Greens Powder
www.**privatelabel**supplement.com/product/**greens_powder**/ ▾
Organic Carrot Juice Powder, Organic Broccoli Juice Powder, Organic Cauliflower
Green Tea Leaf Extract Powder, Quercitin Powder, Blueberry Powder, ...

GREEN PHYTOFOODS POWDER 10 OZ
www.healthgenesis**privatelabel**.com/**green**-**superfoods**-**powder**-10-oz.html ▾
Supplement Facts Serving Size: 1 Level Tablespoon (9.3g) Servings Per Container
Alfalfa Juice Concentrate 700 mg ** Organic Wheat Grass Powder 500 mg ...

Superior Greens Packets on the Go - FoodScience of Vermont
www.foodscienceofvermont.com › Specialty Health Supplements ▾
Interested in private labeling this product? ... Beet Juice Powder, Cauliflower
Powder, Flax Seed Meal, ... Green Tea (Camellia sinensis) Extract 50 mg *.

Spectra Greens - Davinci Laboratories
www.davincilabs.com › Men's, Women's and Specialty Products ▾
Interested in private labeling this product? ... Parsley (Petroselinum crispum) Juice
Powder 200 mg * ... Green Tea (Camellia sinensis) Extract 50 mg *

Green Superfood| Private Label - Vitacap Labs
www.vitacaplabs.com/**green**-**superfood**.html ▾
Green Superfood. Manufacture your own private label greens powder with Vitacap
Labs. Learn how to start your own private label green superfood business

Private Label Superfoods - Evivita
evivita.com/production/**private-label**.../**private-label-superfoods**.html ▾
Feb 11, 2014 - Would you like to expand an existing line or start a new private label of

How To Find Private Labels/How to find products and suppliers

Method # 1 - Alibaba

http://www.alibaba.com/private-label-manufacturers.html

Alibaba is one of the most common ways to get Private Label
Products.

The process is basically the same with WWB. You find a supplier, a
product and contact them.

Beware though, some suppliers really sucks...sorry, there's just no word to describe their products and services,,.. it sucks. I'm not saying that you couldn't find a decent supplier on Alibaba, but I tend to find quality suppliers on WWB more often.

Here are some guideline to follow for you to find great suppliers in Alibaba.

Response Rate

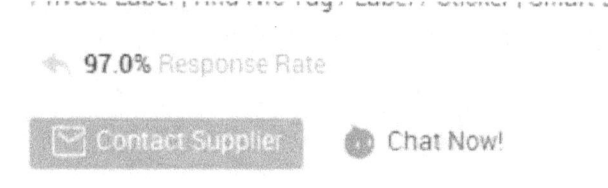

Higher response rate means they actually care about their customers.

Gold Supplier Badge

Some companies who have longer gold badge tends to provide better products and better deals.

On Time Shipment

You always want suppliers who ship their products on time.

If you really wanted to private label your products, I recommend that you spend a few hours talking to as many private label companies as possible. You never know when you gonna find the best deal.

Having a Private label product gives you an identity, a brand that you can market and build, which sells you more products in the long run. It does have a higher cost compared to just re-selling products first. If you're just getting started and have no cash. I suggest that you start with the 4th or 5th method that I will teach you.

So how do you know if a supplier is a WINNER or a LOSER?

Look for feedback

You can also try to search for people who have tried their products. maybe you have an old friend who runs his own private label business. Catch up with him and ask for their opinion. Also, you can attend marketing events by people like you who wants to sells on Amazon or are already selling on Amazon. Also, a google search for that company will go a long way.

Warning: Never, ever order a full batch of products (usually $5,000 - $20,000) unless you have already tested the market.

Re-selling

Alibaba can also be used for reselling products.

For alibaba, what I usually do is just go through different categories and find different products.

I decided to go for baby products

Now, on Amazon I found a product that is selling quite well.

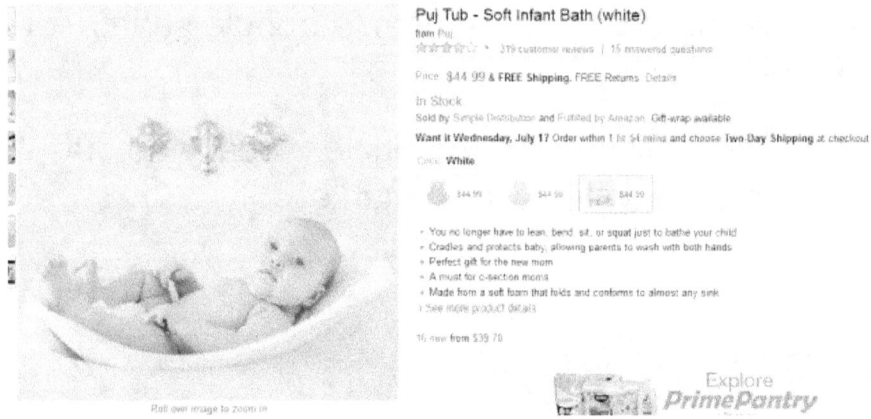

This one sells for $44.99, What you can do is find similar products on Alibaba. Again, it doesn't have to be exactly the same, but it has to be good quality product. The rationale behind it is that if people are buying that kind of product on Amazon, then you can probably sell the same "type" of product as well.

Look at what I found,

This one sells for $2-$5 per piece when you order them.

You can probably sell it for $20 a piece.

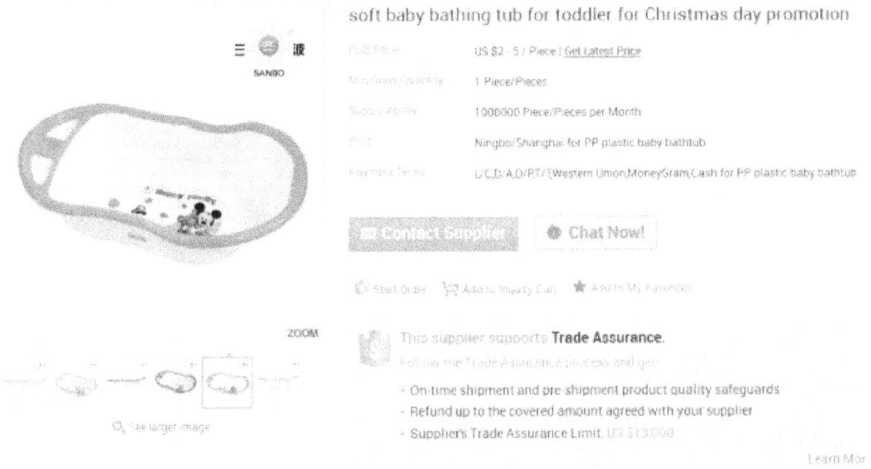

soft baby bathing tub for toddler for Christmas day promotion

Just rinse and repeat the process. Not all products will be gold, you just have to keep digging and maybe you'll find one that will make you the most profit.

Method # 2 - Ebay

One of the best ways to profit in Amazon is to find undervalued products on Ebay. Some people might think that Ebay is dying, Ha! they are wrong, there's still a lot of people making money on Ebay. It might not be as profitable as before, but it's still a money maker for smart marketers.

What you can do is rebrand a product by taking better pictures on different angles and having better packages.

Also, don't be afraid to sort of change the strategy by buying on Amazon and selling on ebay instead. If you found an opportunity to profit, go on and take advantage of this. Some products are much cheaper in Amazon compared to Ebay and vice versa.

How to find awesome products on Ebay

Once you chose your plan of attack (chapter 2), go to ebay and find products that are similar to your chosen market.
Let's say I decided to go target "women's accessories" on the top 2,000.

I found this one on ebay selling for $9.60 per piece.

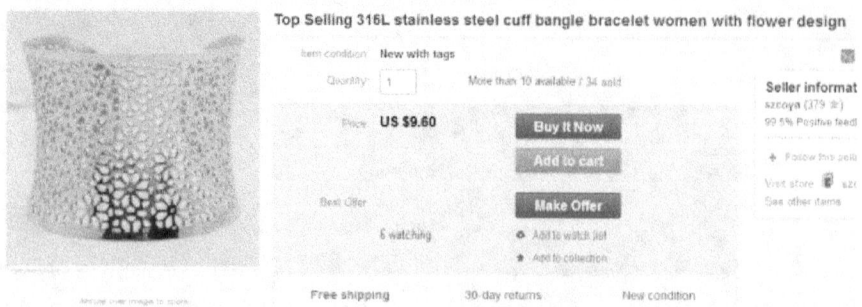

What I'll do next is find similar products on Amazon that sells for a higher price.

Please note that it doesn't really have to be the same product. It just have to be a bit similar. If that product is selling on Ebay, then it must be selling also on Amazon.

The 4th item below seems similar to the one on Ebay but not really the same. It's selling for $15, we can make a good $3 profit per item. Not a lot but if you can sell just a piece a day, that's an extra $90 a month. It can add up pretty fast especially if you're selling a bunch of items in that niche.

Now, we are not sure if that item is going to make sales because it's not really a best seller, but still, I hope that you get the gist of the ebay method.

Here's another example, but instead we're going to sell on Ebay.

search term : remote control helicopter

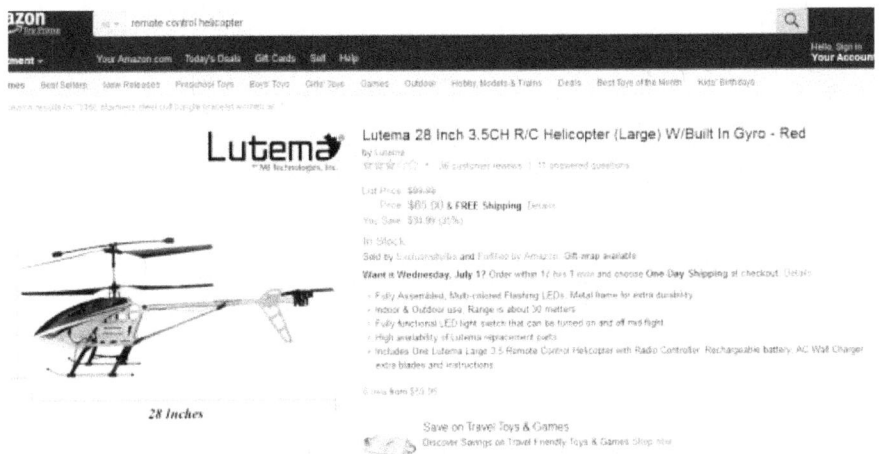

It sells for $65 on Amazon

And on Ebay… $80 per item.

Do you think you could make a profit by doing this alone? Of course.

Method # 3 - Walmart
http://www.walmart.com (go to the website and look for discounts)

Another awesome source of products is walmart. It's cheap and they give free shipping. What I do is find sales and discounts and then make sure that there is a market for it on Amazon.

Ex.

I found this on a discount on Walmart

Backyard Grill 18.5" Charcoal Grill, Black

$22.00

When I searched for charcoal grills on Amazon, I found the one below.

This one is almost the same product (in fact, the one from walmart is much bigger and cheaper)

This sells for $32, I would like to think that I can make a profit by buying the $22 product on Walmart (w/ free shipping) and then sell it on Amazon for $32 or more.

Charcoal Grill, Backyard Grill 17.5". Grills up to 15 Burgers. Porcelain enamel cooking grid. With 2 plastic wheels for easy transport. Dimensions: 18.31"L x 5.22"W x 18.5"H
by Backyard Grill

Price: $32.41 & FREE Shipping

In stock
Ships from and sold by Connect Buy.
Estimated Delivery Date: July 6 - 9 when you choose Expedited at checkout

- 282 sq in grilling surface
- Silver enamel tube legs and bottom wire mesh
- 2 plastic wheels enable easy transport
- Equipped with a bottom storage shelf for easy access to charcoal and other items
- Barbecue grill has a black porcelain hinged lid

17 new from $20.92

Here's another example.

I found this one on the VALUE OF THE DAY tab.

$12.99

List price $45.99 You Save $33.00

Coleman Sevylor Specialists - Two-Person
Inflatable Boat

Quick Look

it sells for $12.99

And if you search on Amazon

"coleman inflatable boats"

you'll see that it sells for $46.71

If find something similar to that and sell it for $30, you would still be able to make a good $10-$15 profit.

I hope that I have expanded your imagination when it comes to finding products. It is probably the most important skills to master if you want to succeed in this business.

4 - TTNET

I love this resource. They can give you a lot of different products to choose from and different choices of the product's origin country. Simply search for your product and you'll find a lot of suppliers ready to talk to you via email/chat/phone.

Hot Products: Baby Gift Sets   Bicycle Accessories   Axe   Bicycle Helmet

If you want to search by country or categories, you can simply choose one and go on with your research.

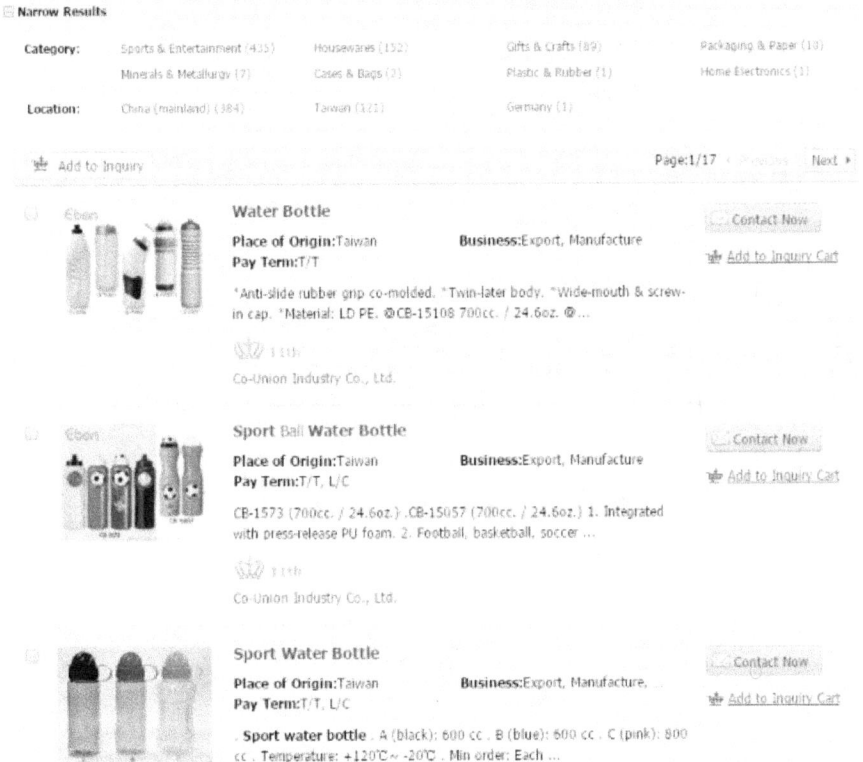

When you are looking for a supplier, make sure that you only deal with the MANUFACTURER and not a trading company.
Like this one (I can't confirm it but this one is not a direct manufacturer, they're just wholesalers)

Sports Water Bottle

High Quality Photo - Sports Water Bottle

Product Category	Sport Water Bottles
Min. Order	300 Pieces
Unit Price	US $ 0.9-1.0 / Piece
Country of Origin	Shanghai , Shanghai , China (mainland)
Product Packing Way	OPP bags
Payment Term	T/T, Western Union
Delivery Port	Shanghai
Sales Method	Export, Wholesale

✉ Contact Now

🛒 Put In Inquiry Cart   🔍 Find Similar Product

8+1 0

AGAIN, ONLY DEAL WITH THE MANUFACTURER.
Wholesalers & Trading companies will add 15-20% to your total Cost of goods sold. Not cool.
In the product listing, you will see their company name.
Always open this before contacting them.

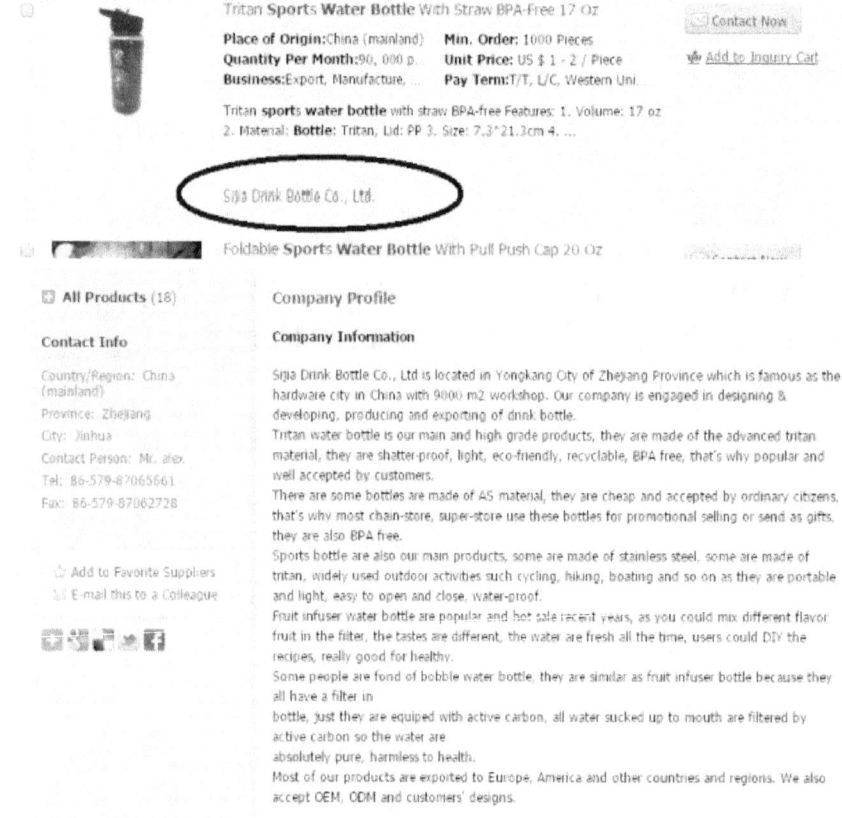

Tritan **Sports Water Bottle** With Straw BPA-Free 17 Oz

Place of Origin: China (mainland) **Min. Order:** 1000 Pieces
Quantity Per Month:90, 000 p... **Unit Price:** US $ 1 - 2 / Piece
Business: Export, Manufacture, ... **Pay Term:**T/T, L/C, Western Uni...

Tritan **sports water bottle** with straw BPA-free Features: 1. Volume: 17 oz
2. Material: **Bottle:** Tritan, Lid: PP 3. Size: 7.3*21.3cm 4. ...

Sijia Drink Bottle Co., Ltd.

☑ Contact Now

👍 Add to Inquiry Cart

Foldable **Sports Water Bottle** With Pull Push Cap 20 Oz

📋 **All Products** (18)

Contact Info

Country/Region: China (mainland)
Province: Zhejiang
City: Jinhua
Contact Person: Mr. alex
Tel: 86-579-87065661
Fax: 86-579-87062728

☆ Add to Favorite Suppliers
✉ E-mail this to a Colleague

Company Profile

Company Information

Sijia Drink Bottle Co., Ltd is located in Yongkang City of Zhejiang Province which is famous as the hardware city in China with 9000 m2 workshop. Our company is engaged in designing & developing, producing and exporting of drink bottle.
Tritan water bottle is our main and high grade products, they are made of the advanced tritan material, they are shatter-proof, light, eco-friendly, recyclable, BPA free, that's why popular and well accepted by customers.
There are some bottles are made of AS material, they are cheap and accepted by ordinary citizens, that's why most chain-store, super-store use these bottles for promotional selling or send as gifts. they are also BPA free.
Sports bottle are also our main products, some are made of stainless steel, some are made of tritan, widely used outdoor activities such cycling, hiking, boating and so on as they are portable and light, easy to open and close, water-proof.
Fruit infuser water bottle are popular and hot sale recent years, as you could mix different flavor fruit in the filter, the tastes are different, the water are fresh all the time, users could DIY the recipes, really good for healthy.
Some people are fond of bobble water bottle, they are similar as fruit infuser bottle because they all have a filter in
bottle, just they are equiped with active carbon, all water sucked up to mouth are filtered by active carbon so the water are
absolutely pure, harmless to health.
Most of our products are exported to Europe, America and other countries and regions. We also accept OEM, ODM and customers' designs.

Read everything that you can about this company, especially if you plan to do a lot of business with them.

It would also be smart to Google search them and find their websites. Most of these guys in TTNET don't show their website. So you have to do more research.

Also, it would be nice to know their specialty. You only want the best and your customers deserve only the best.

If you don't have a product idea yet, you can reverse engineer the website and look for different items.

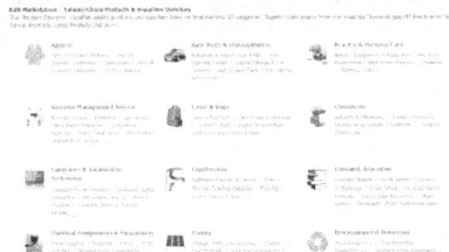

You can also email support and ask for their best categories or the categories with the most suppliers. More products in a certain category just mean more people are looking for it.

6 – HKTDC
Another awesome place to find products is HKTDC.

They have a lot of suppliers from Hongkong, China and Taiwan.

It's pretty much the same as TTNE, but bigger, you just have to search for your product and look at different suppliers that may have your product.

When you do your research, make sure that you tick on the MANUFACTURER only.

You may also want to consider the "credentials" bar and check out their certificates and verifications. It's really hard to explain all of it in details but I suggest that you ask customer support to explain this to you. I swear, it's worth asking and taking 15 minutes of your time to read all of those details.

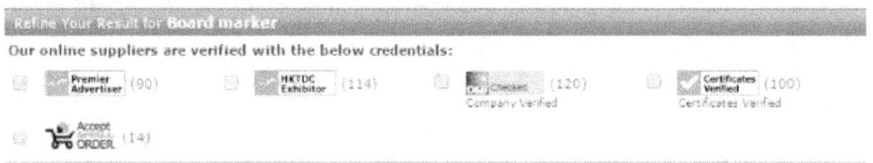

You can also click on those certifications to know what it means.

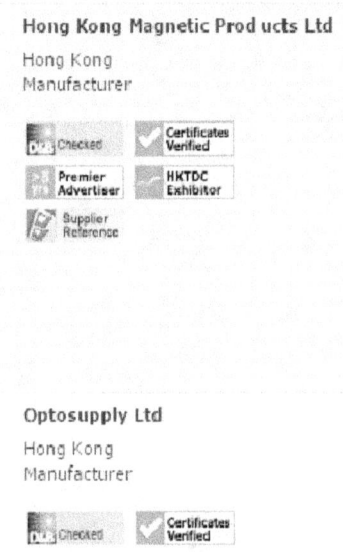

Optosupply Ltd

Hong Kong
Manufacturer

The more certifications they have,, the more likely they are to be a legit company.

Don't tick the ACCEPT SMALL ORDER button even if you're only planning to order a small amount of quantity. They will charge you more per item if you chose those suppliers. I will teach you how to negotiate MOQ later. If they really won't accept a lower Minimum order quantity (MOQ), then that's where you consider those

who accept small order quantities.

 (12)

Don't forget to check more details about the company.

SMD LED Light

Min. Order: 10,000 pc(s)
Production Lead Time: 12-14 week(s)

Optosupply Ltd
Hong Kong

her Matching Items (6) See All

7-   >

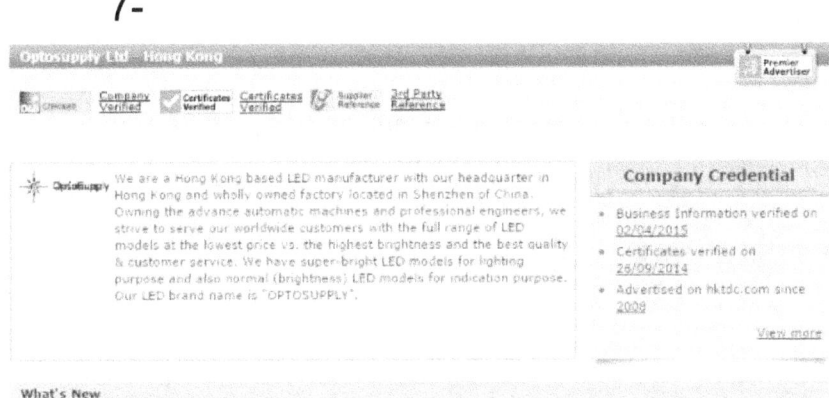

Optosupply Ltd - Hong Kong

We are a Hong Kong based LED manufacturer with our headquarter in Hong Kong and wholly owned factory located in Shenzhen of China. Owning the advance automatic machines and professional engineers, we strive to serve our worldwide customers with the full range of LED models at the lowest price vs. the highest brightness and the best quality & customer service. We have super-bright LED models for lighting purpose and also normal (brightness) LED models for indication purpose. Our LED brand name is "OPTOSUPPLY".

Company Credential

- Business Information verified on 02/04/2015
- Certificates verified on 26/09/2014
- Advertised on hktdc.com since 2009

View more

What's New

December 24, 2011   phosphor mixer and high power led bin sorter

Chapter 4 – Writing a Product Listing

So you found a product, ordered and received it. It's now time to sell it. For you to make a lot of profits, you have to create a product listing that really highlights the best features and benefits of your product. Also, it must be AMAZON optimized so it'll appear much higher on amazon search engine.

Follow these simple guidelines to make your product listing ready for action.

Photos

Always use high quality photos. A bad photo will make your product appear unprofessional. Also, always look white background.

In addition, when uploading your pictures, change their file names into your keywords.

Titles

Write detailed product title. It helps in Amazon optimization and it makes your product stand out.

Instead of saying...

bad - Helicopter Remote Control (Red)
good - UDI U818A 2.4GHz 4 CH 6 Axis Gyro RC Quadcopter with Camera RTF Mode 2 (red) - Easy to use and control - even for kids and beginners

Make it detailed and also add some benefits.

Benefits are - *Easy to use and control - even for kids and beginners*

Features are - *Axis Gyro RC Quadcopter with Camera RTF Mode 2 (red) - the physical attributes of the product*

Description

Never rush on the creation of your description. By writing a thorough description, you'll be able to explain your product features and benefits much better. Also, it can help you rank in more keywords not included in your title.

In addition, take full advantage of the HTML amazon description feature. It helps it making your description look better and change font size, bold, etc.

Here are some basics that you can use.

B - BOLDS a phrase, used to define some words.
P - Defines a paragraph
BR - Adds line break

Here's an example on how to use this on a listing.

<p><b> Why Choose This Product</b></p>

<p> - Discraft 175 gram Ultra Star Sport Disc</br>
-The world standard for the sport of Ultimate</br>
-Official and exclusive disc of the USA Ultimate Championship Series since 1991.</br>
-Listed among the 31 things all men should own by Esquire magazine</br>
-175 grams</br>
-Foil color on the disc will vary</p>

UPC Code

Amazon requires sellers to provide a 12 digit Universal Product Code assigned for every product. This was a huge problem in the past since not every supplier provide UPC.

You can get a barcode for $1 a piece

Chapter 5 - Shipping via FBA step by step

This chapter will be short and sweet :)

So you got your product, you've created your product listing draft. It's time to make your product available for sale via FBA.

Step 1 - Send Your Product To An Amazon Fulfillment Center

- Go to your Amazon Seller Central and create your official product listing.
- Print the labels provided by Amazon or use FBA's Label Service.
- Use Amazon's shipping to get discount or chose your own carrier if you want

Step 2 - Amazon stores your products, now ready for shipping

- Amazon receives your product. They scan and measure your product.
- Using Amazon's integrated tracking system, you monitor your product inventory.

Step 3 - Amazon does everything else for you. The shipping, the customer service etc. Just make sure that you are enrolled on FBA program.

FBA Quick Start

You can add Fulfillment by Amazon to your Selling on Amazon account quickly and easily following these simple steps:

1. Go to **Inventory** > **Manage Inventory**
2. Select a product you would like to include as an FBA listing by checking the box next to it in the far left column.
3. From the **Actions** pull-down menu, select "Change to Fulfilled by Amazon"
4. On the next page, click the **Convert** button.
5. Follow the directions for creating your first shipment.

Illustration:

source:www.amvsmlm.com

Frequently Asked Questions

If you can write a FAQ for your product, do it! The more questions you have, the better.

SEARCH TERMS

Put the top 5 main keywords that you are targeting.

Step 5 – Facebook Product Advertising for Beginners

What I'll teach you in this chapter are just the basics but it'll still be useful to you especially if you're just an absolute beginner.

You have to create a facebook page first and then create an ad.

Then define your audience.

Really ask yourself, who will be buying my products?

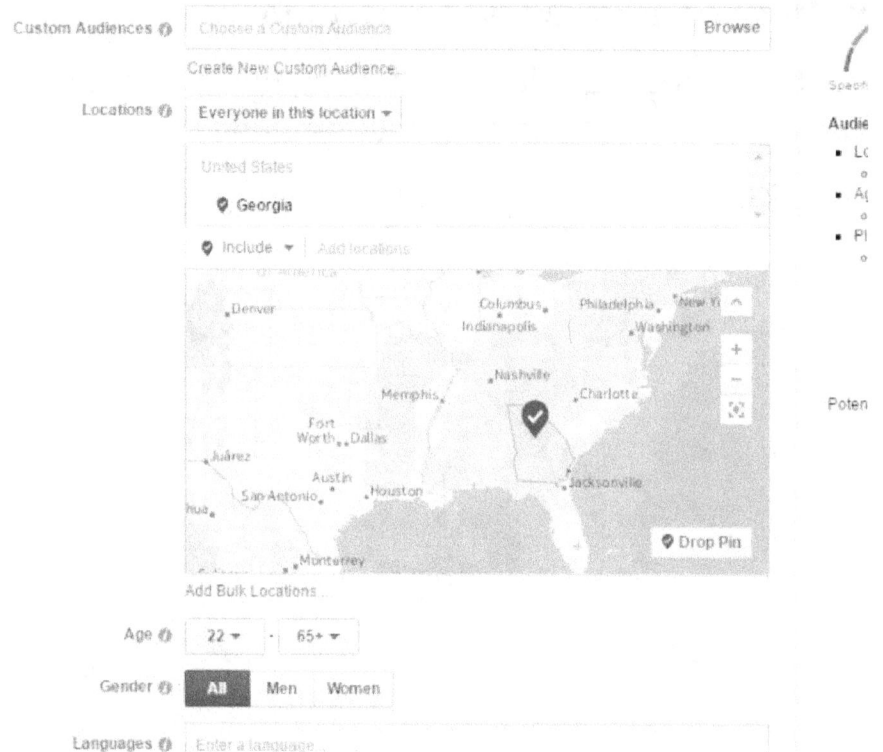

Then put some related interest.

If you're selling some Star Wars related item. Then put star wars as interest.

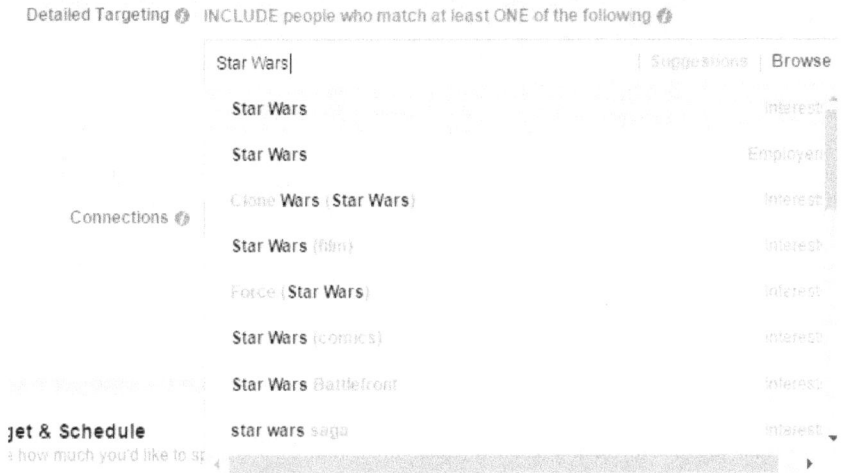

Then set your daily budget.

Budget ℹ️   Daily Budget ▾ |10.00

Leave this as is.

Then click
Choose ad creative

Choose Ad Creative

REMOVE all of these except DESKTOP.

✓ Desktop News Feed	Remove
✓ Mobile News Feed	Remove

See Feature Phone Preview   See Smartphone Preview

View in Native App

✓ Instagram	Remove
✓ Audience Network ⓘ	Remove
✓ Desktop Right Column	Remove

Then put your image, headline and description.

There's no magic formula for your headline and description.

Just make it as cut and dry as possible. Then put your product url.

• Image   Video

Image ⓘ

Change Image   Crop Image

 ~ 900 × 900

For questions and more information, see the Facebook
Ad Guidelines.

Headline ⓘ   14

Star Wars Yoda Toy 50% Off

Description (optional) ⓘ   -5

May the force be with you

Destination URL ⓘ

amazonurl.com   ✕

Then place order and track your results! That's it!

Review Order   Place Order

Conclusion

Thanks for reading this book.

Hopefully, you get your money's worth.

Treat the information in this book as a POTENTIAL.

It's still up to you if you'll properly use it or just let it pass by.

You know, I'm really bad at writing these book conclusions.

I guess what I'm saying is just take the goddamn action!

Seriously, just take step 1,,, and step 2 and so on.

Nothing will happen if you just keep worrying about stuff.

Just take the first step and let it take you from there.

Good luck!

NO CAPITAL DROPSHIPPING

How to Create and Grow Your Own E-Commerce Dropshipping Business
Without Spending a Single Dime on Inventory and Advertising

Erik Malik

w/ Andy Black

TABLE OF CONTENTS

Introduction

There are literally thousands of ways to make money but somehow, you end up reading this book about dropshipping.

I wrote this book for 2 kinds of people.

1 – The one looking for a way to start a business without capital whatsoever

2 – The one who is willing to do the work required to succeed

If you match both of the description, then this book is for you.

Online dropshipping is basically selling products that you don't have at the moment and then ordering them to the original seller once your buyer pays you the money.

So you're just a middleman in this situation.

You don't have to worry about inventories and all that stuff.

You only job is to market your products!

That's it.

Don't forget this line.

Your only real job is to sell the product.

On the next few chapters, I'm gonna show you a simple way to make money via what I call NO CAPITAL DROPSHIPPING.

It means even if you don't have a single dime in your bank account, you can still apply what you'll learn from this book.

My only wish for you is that you don't take the SIMPLE but useful information in this book.

Sounds fair?

Let's get started.

Step 1 - Find a Product on Ebay & Aliexpress

The 1st step to a successful dropshipping business is to find a profitable product.

So how do we know that the product we'll choose is likely to make money or not?

Simple, just follow my criterion that has been proven to weed out the weak products.

#1 – Price should be $10-60

It should be an impulse buy. Our website doesn't have the trust that other sites like Amazon have.

The lower the price the easier it is to sell. However, this only applies for beginner sellers like you.

#2 – It should be light

We want something that has free shipping on Ebay or Aliexpress. Most of the time, light products are the ones that has free shipping.

#3 – Other people are already buying it on Aliexpress.com or Ebay.com

We can easily see this one of the salespage of the product. I'll teach you how to do this later.

Just follow these 3 criterion and you are most likely to find good products to sell on your own website.

Now, it's time to find some money makers!

Method # 1 – WATCHCOUNT.com (EBAY)

http://www.watchcount.com/

Not too many people do this but the first thing I want you to do is go to FREE SHIPPING section.

By doing this, we already satisfied are second criteria.

Now, we only have to find something between 10-60 bucks and make sure that there are people already buying that product.

Find something that you are interested in at first so you'll have a more enjoyable time choosing a product to sell.

This marvel deadpool caught my attention so I'm gonna look at the numbers and see if I can sell this and still make a profit off of it.

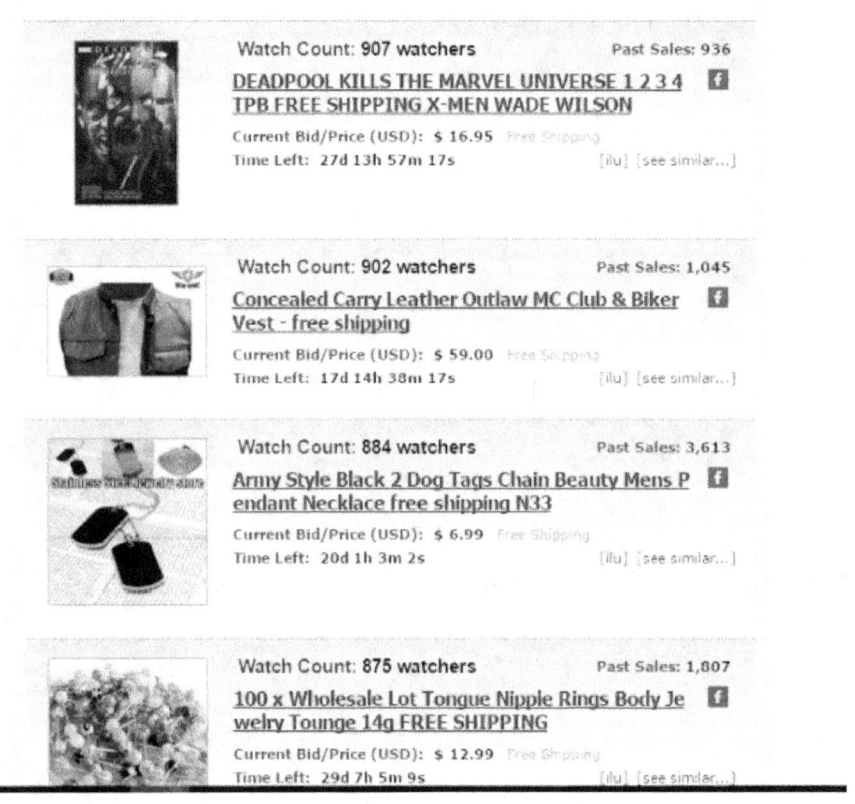

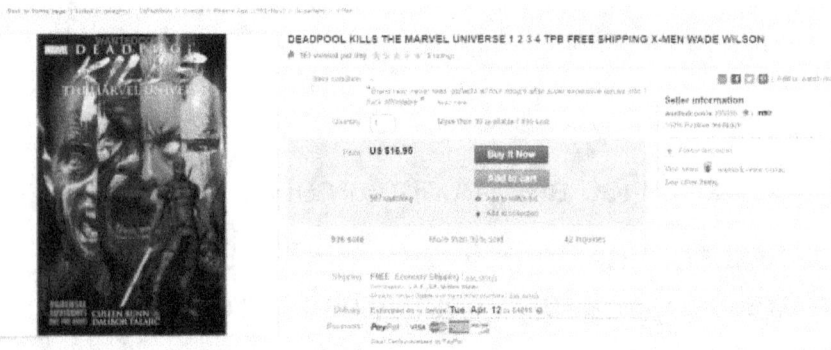

-    It has over 936 sold items.
-    It has 9 star ratings
-    The product is only 16.95
-    It has free shipping
-    Also, there's a passionate crowd (marvel comics fans) that I can easily target online

Based on those things, I will choose this product as one of my main products to sell on my website.

Also, if possible make sure that you find other sellers that may be selling it for much lower prices.

You can just simply repeat the process over and over again when trying to find a profitable product.

1 - Go to watchcount

http://watchcount.com

2 – Look at free shipping

What's Hot on eBay?

Free Shipping! Gymboree gold coin baseball card le Titanic Toys/Hobbies Tickets Harley Davidson Disne yang Elvis Presley iPhone Everything Else plasma T Deer Free Shipping! - Most Watched/Popular on el

3 – Find something that interest you

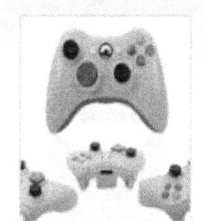

Watch Count: **777 watchers**   Past Sales: 1,735

Pink Wireless Game Remote Controller for Micros oft Xbox360 Console Free Shipping

Current Bid/Price (USD): $ 25.99 Free Shipping

Time Left: 27d 7h 29m 21s   [ilu] [see similar...]

Watch Count: **747 watchers**   Past Sales: 2

BRAND NEW ATT U-verse S20-S1A Programmable Universal Remote FREE SHIPPING

Current Bid/Price (USD): $ 6.50 Free Shipping

Time Left: 11d 21h 13m 42s   [ilu] [see similar...]

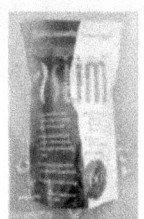

Watch Count: **745 watchers**   Past Sales: 5,983

Plexus Slim - 30 Day Supply PINK DRINK Weight L oss Packets - FREE SHIPPING

Current Bid/Price (USD): $ 77.95 Free Shipping

Time Left: 3d 19h 19m 35s   [ilu] [see similar...]

Watch Count: **740 watchers**   Past Sales: 375

4 – Look at the numbers

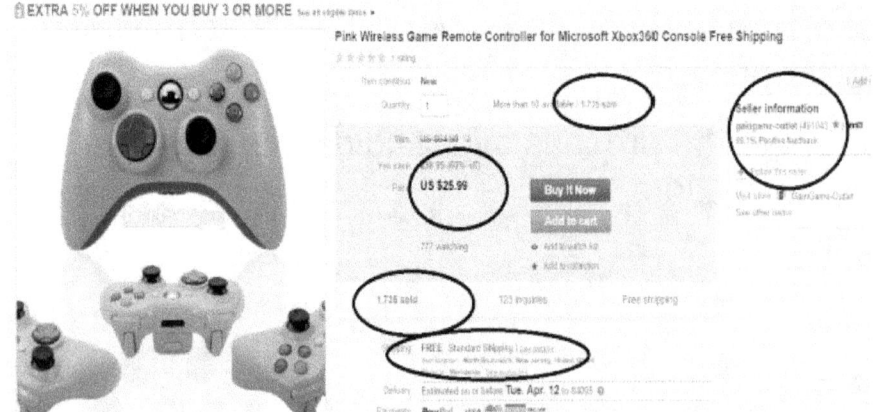

If they make sense, then choose it!

It's that simple!

Method #2 – ALIEXPRESS

Aliexpress.com is a website under alibaba.com

It's basically the retailer part of the bigger company Alibaba

For you to find great products on Aliexpress, I need you to follow the same criteria when choosing something to sell.

#1 – Price should be $10-60

#2 – It should be light

#3 – Other people are already buying it on Aliexpress.com or Ebay.com (numbers should make sense)

So go to the home page and click BESTSELLING

By choosing products from the bestseller category, we already satisfied criteria #3

Now, we just have to find something that matches criteria #1 and criteria #2

Just simply browse your way to the best seller and find a product that you will buy yourself.

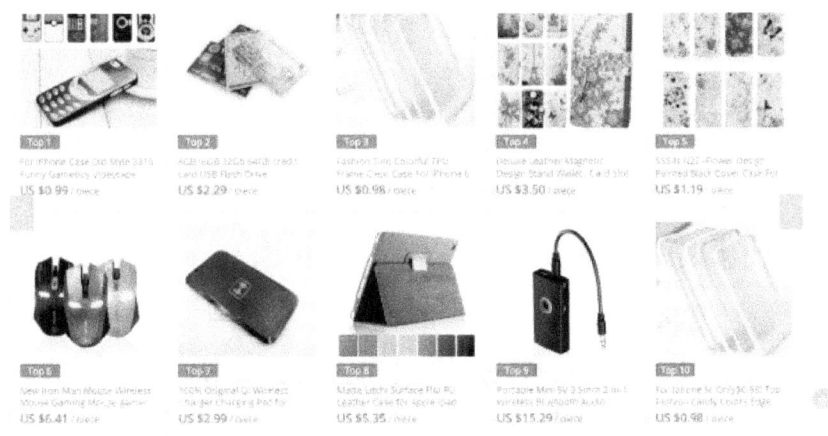

For me, it's this Iron Man wireless mouse.

It looks cool and it seems like it has high value.

Now, I have to check if the numbers make sense.

Are people actually buying this and is there free or at least cheap shipping?

This one's looking really good.

Look at the numbers and data I got.

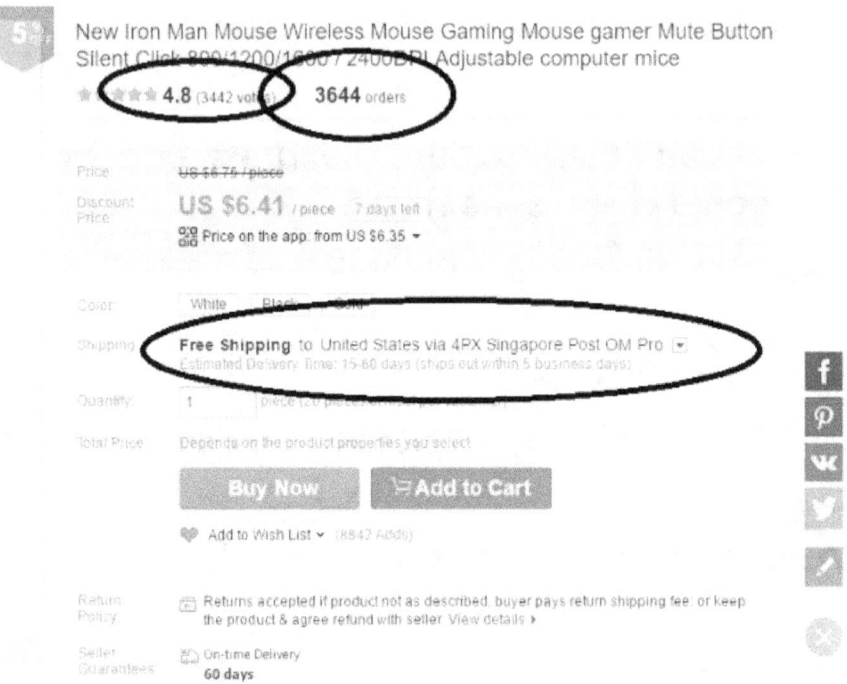

- It has 4.8 rating (which is really good)
- It already has 3644 orders so far
- It has free shipping
- There's a huge market for gaming mouse
- There are legions of Iron Man followers around the world

With these things in mind, I think it's safe to say that this product is a winner!

Once we chose our product, the next step that we need to do is to create a website and a landing page!

Step 2 - Create a Landing Page (Blogger)

The next step is to go to BLOGER.com and log in on your gmail account.

Create a NEW BLOG.

Then click NEW POST.

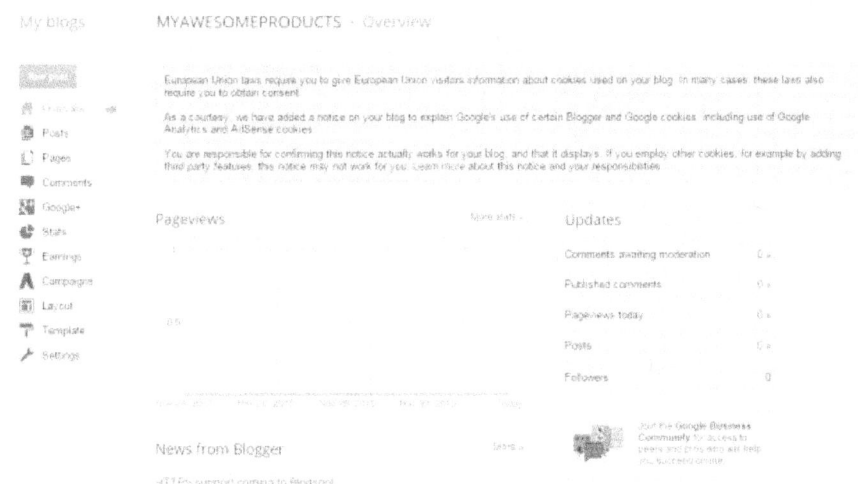

Just get your product description and product pictures from ALIEXPRESS where you got your product.

Then just copy paste it. Seriously, that it ☺

Don't over complicate the process, they're already selling it for years and they must have tested their sales description already.

Say I chose a product about CAMPING WHISTLE, here's how I would create my landing page.

LIMITED OFFER – 20% OFF!

10pcs Mixed Aluminum Emergency Survival Whistle Key chain For Camping & Hiking

(FREE SHIPPING ANYWHERE IN THE U.S.)

NEVER LET YOUR KID OR SOMEONE YOU CARE ABOUT BE IN DANGER EVER AGAIN.

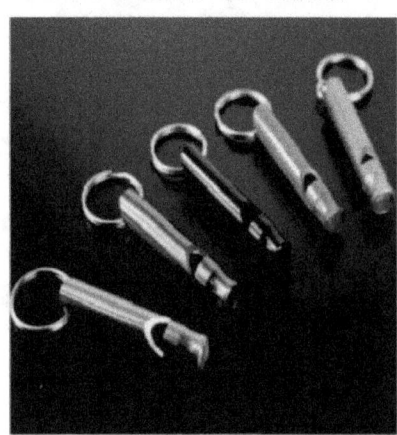

Description

Description

- Quantity 10pcs (color will ship to you at random)
- Materials Aluminium Alloy
-Mainly Colors mixed as shown
-Approx Size length:49mm dia:9mm
-Shape Aluminum Emergency Survival Whistle Key Chain Camping
-Measure Conversion 1mm=0.0393 inch 1 inch=25.4 mm
Item Usage
-A Very Nice Aluminum Emergency Survival Whistle Key Chain Camping,fit outdoor
activity, camping, fishing, hiking, traveling, key-chain etc !

This product sells for $8
+ $5 shipping on Amazon
(BUT ONLY FOR 3PIECES)

For this offer – GRAB 10 PIECES and
GET IT FOR ~~16.99~~ 13.99 TODAY!

w/ 100% 7 DAY MONEY BACK GUARANTEE

VISA   AMEX   PayPal

Additional information:

If your shipping information is different from your paypal/credit card address, kindly put
it as note on the checkout page.

You can create something like this just by creating a NEW PAGE.

The buy button is just a picture I got from Google and then I put my merchant paypal link into it.
You can easily create a merchant link if you already have a paypal. Too be honest, I just search it on Youtube so I'm pretty sure you can do the same. Search for "buy now button paypal". Once you created that buy button link, you'll just copy the code from paypal and paste in the BUY BUTTON picture as a link.

I recommend that you just copy what I tried to do on the images above. You can never go wrong with that landing page.

What makes a landing page convert.

Here are some things that you need to consider when you create your landing page.

1 – Use a headline, something that will caught their attention.

2 – Call out your target market (see my example above) (*never let your kid…*)

3 – Give them the benefits an features of your product

4 – Put a call to action (buy now button)

5 - Make it as simple as possible

6 – If you have limited supplies, then tell them about it.

Step 3 - Sell via FB Fan Page

Facebook is the big daddy of all social medias.

If you're not using it yet then I have no idea how'd you survive :)

The free way to advertise on Facebook is through Facebook Fan Pages.

I will teach the proper profile (business page) creation first then I'll teach you some tactics to use in this traffic source.

Facebook Profile Creation

Here is the step by step process for creating an amazing fan page.

I will assume that you already have a Facebook account, if you haven't registered yet, just go to Facebook.com and sign up for a free account.

Step 1 – Create A Page

Step 2 – Choose A Type Of Organization

Make sure that you put your business name and the correct category for your new page

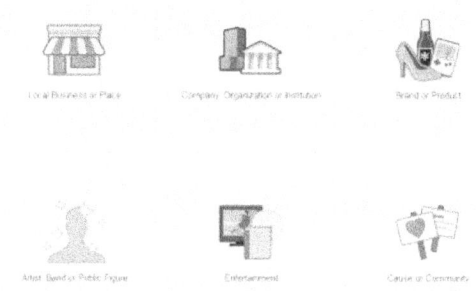

Step 3 – About

Write a brief description of your blog.

What do you do? What are your specialties?

Say I have a blog about fashion design.

I would write something like the one below.

Step 4 – Profile Picture

For your page's profile picture, make sure that you put your company logo.

I usually just skip the Add to favorites part and go straight to "Preferred Audience""

Step 5 – Preferred Audience

For this part, carefully think about who are the majority of your customers.

- their country
- their age
- the things they "like" or their "interests"

Do not skip this part.

This is important because you want to target not just a lot of people but rather the right people for your business/product.

Click SAVE to continue

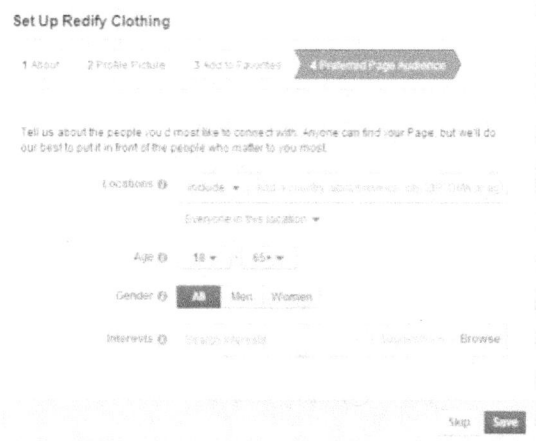

Step 6 – Cover Photo

The last step for basic fan page creation is to add your cover photo.

Do not leave your cover photo blank.

It's unprofessional and it's ugly.

Make your cover photo simple and clean. Feature your product if you can.

HOT TIP: You can add special promotion details in your cover photo, a lot of people usually look at the cover once they land in the page.

Here are some examples of my favorite covers.

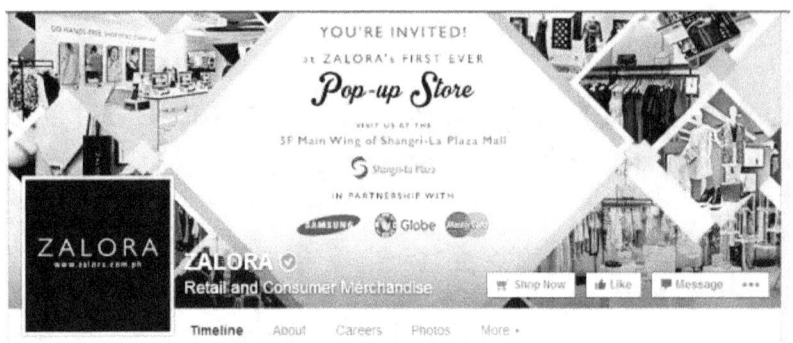

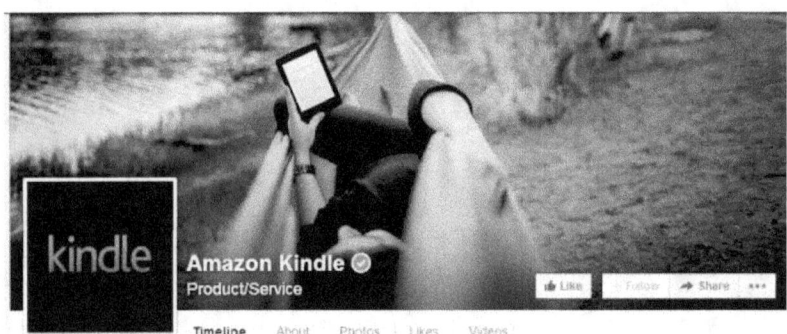

On Posting Content

There are many ways to post content in your fan page but the one thing I will NEVER ever do is to just sell my products.

You may want to provide some insights or value before you sell anything.

Types of Content To Post

A. Text

This is the most basic for a post. It's still an effective way to communicate but the bad thing is that it is very forgettable.

When was the last time you read a long text post?

B. Pictures

Posting a picture is a very effective way to communicate with your audience.

You can also create TEXT in pictures so instead of just posting a text post, you'll just post a picture.

Here is an example of a text to picture post from the page "The Millionaire Fast Lane" (which is a book)

It has 722 likes and 295 shares.

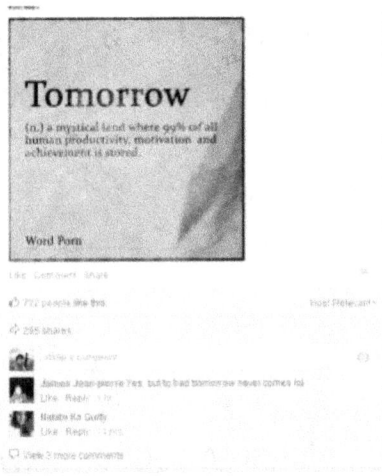

C. Videos

Videos are also an effective way to talk to your customers. It takes a little bit more effort but if you have something interesting to say, then they will watch your video.

You can try these simple suggestions to get them to watch your video

- make it HD quality video

- Giveaway prizes

- give away discounts and in the video, explain what they need to do to get that discounts

- Hire celebrities. Don't worry, it doesn't have to be an award winning artist.

How To Get Facebook Fans

What I'm going to reveal to you are the simplest but the most effective ways to build your FB fan pages. Put these suggestions into action and you're going to increase your customers by at least 20% in 2- 6 months.

#1 – Friends, Family and Current Customers

If I am just starting out, what I would do is I will reach out to my friends, family and even current customers.

Email them or personally talk to them. You can also message them on Facebook to like your new business page.

If you can get 20-50 likes then that a pretty good starting point.

#2 – Fiverr

Another way to get facebook fans is to promote your fan page by using Fiverr. These are not highly targeted people but it can help you grow "likes" which can serve as social proof for your business.

(If a lot of people are liking this page then this must be worth "liking" for)

#3 Run a Contest

Running a contest is one of the fastest ways to get more fans on FB.

ALWAYS tell your audience that they will only be eligible to receive the product if they will LIKE and SHARE the content shared.

You can even give away products unrelated to yours but I would suggest that you start with your own.

One of the most famous products to give as a contest prize is an apple product.

HOT TRAFFIC GETTING METHOD Facebook 2.0

Optimize your Facebook for SEO. If you can rank your FB page on Google then you will get more traffic.

A. Optimize Title

If you can, put your keyword in your business page name. If not, make sure that you optimize your description properly.

B. Optimize Description

In your description area, include the following:

- your phone number
- your website
- your complete address
- your keywords (if you're trying to rank for INTERNATIONAL SEO FIRM, then put it on the description)

E.g.: (You can edit your description in the ABOUT page)

Short Description	International SEO Expert
	SEO Glendale Firm
	Seoul SEO
	SEO Charleston
Impressum	Input Impressum for your Page
Long Description	We are International SEO Firm. We even serve
	SEO Glendale, Seoul SEO and other local and
	international clients
Price Range	Unspecified ▼

[Save Changes] Cancel

Step 4 – Optimize for Search Engine Traffic

There are a shit ton of other ways to rank your website on Google but these are the best backlinking tactics to help you rank your sites faster than your competition – for free!

The Power of Backlinks

Just in case you don't know the meaning of a backlink yet, let me explain.

Basically, it's a link (a referral) from one website to another.

Let's say I'm on facebook and I share a youtube video.

I just send a backlink from Facebook to the youtube video.

You get it? Awesome.

BACKLINKING POWER

Let me ask you a question.

Do you believe that you can rank on a competitive market without building backlinks?

HELL NO.

Google relies on backlinks to let them know the authority, relevance and the usefulness of a website.

You shouldn't spam your website with trash backlinks though. You'll get penalize by Google and kick your website out of the Google search engine.

Today, too many people are now *uber* cautious about SEO. They think that quality content is the answer to their Google rankings (or the lack of it). Don't get me wrong, you should have unique and awesome content. It does help you in ranking your websites. But the truth is, BACKLINKS are still KING.

Assuming that two websites have the same quality content and same on page seo stuff; the website with the more powerful backlinks will get a higher Google ranking.

In the following pages, I'll teach you 4 of the best ways to build backlinks for free or at the very least, cheap.

1 – TUMBLR

Tumblr is a high pr social website.

Go to https://www.tumblr.com and register for a free account.

Confirm your account on your email.

After you log in to your account. Click the human shape button on the right side of the blog.

Then click on NEW

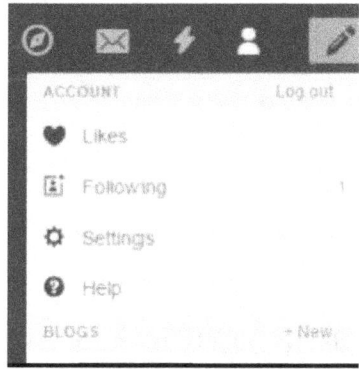

You should see something like this.

Create a title that is related to your target keyword or your company brand. If you are targeting the keyword "Dallas SEO Services" then use the title Dallas Seo Services and the url as "dallasseoservices.tumblr.com

If it's not available, use something that is related to the term like Dallasseoservicesblog.tumblr.com

After creating your blog. Write or outosurce a 500 word article that contains your main keywords then link it to your money site.

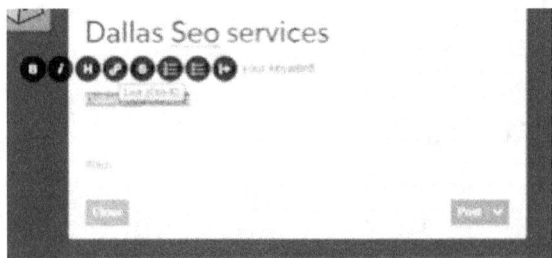

Your keyword should be linking to your money site.

2 – GUEST POSTING

To do a guest post, you must have a pretty decent blog first. Most blogs won't allow you to guest post if you are just new in the industry.
To find a blog to guest post with, simply do a good search –
TOPIC + GUEST POST, you'll find some paid and free blog to guest post with.
Make sure that you have a quality content to share first before asking anyone for a guest post.
At the end of the post, you'll just build a link to your site and voila! you're done.

3 – BUY IT

If you don't want to spend a lot of time manually building backlinks, I suggest that you buy them on fiverr.

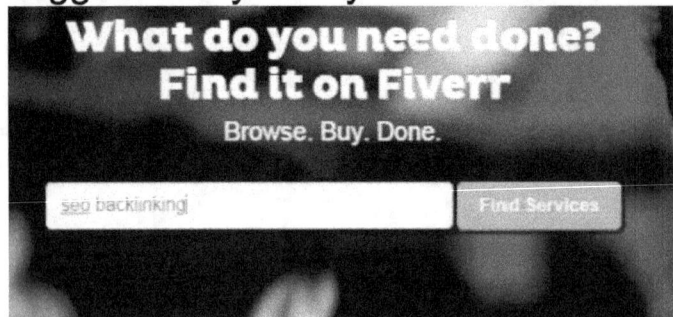

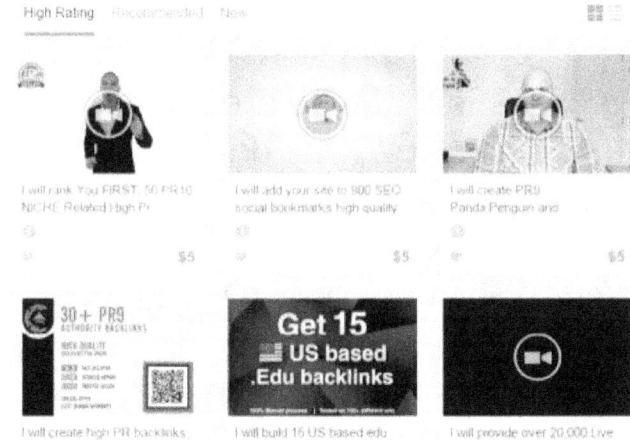

There's a lot of service out there for as low as $5. Just make sure that you follow the backlinking structure that I will suggest you do. (on the next chapter)

Another awesome place to buy seo services is through source market.

It's a website by a famous seo guru Alex Becker.

SOURCE MARKET (< -yes, this is an affiliate link)

It's a market specifically created for SEO.

I don't have a product for sale here yet, but I'll probably start selling soon. SO watch out for my services – REDIFY SEO.

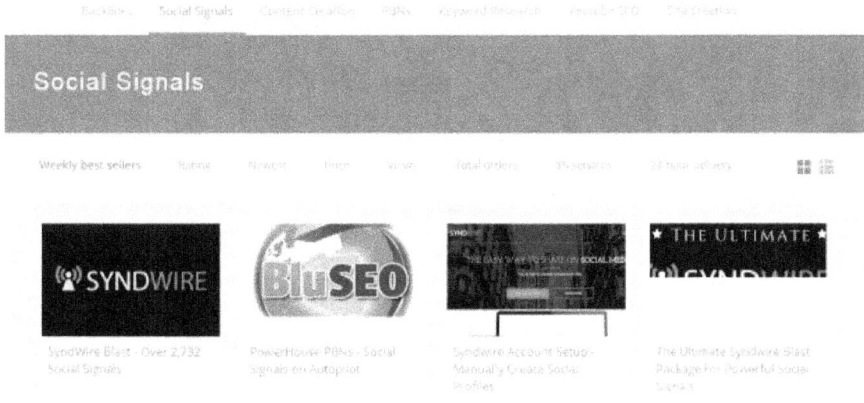

4 – AUDIO SHARING SITES

What I like about audio sharing websites is that they are not as highly moderated compared to other sites. Now, that doesn't mean you can just spam the hell out of these websites.

The first thing that you need to do is to record an audio. Just say whatever you want to say about your website. A one minute audio would do.

You can use http://vocaroo.com to record your own voice. Save it as mp3 file.

Now, go to these audio sharing sites and register for a free account. Simply upload your audios and don't forget to put your website or a backlink to your profile or to the audio you are uploading.

http://bandcamp.com
http://reverbnation.com
http://8tracks.com
http://sutros.com
http://soundcloud.com
http://yourlisten.com
http://mobypicture.com
http://playlist.net
http://wearehunted.com

Followers   Following   Tracks
966K   10   318

Join the conversation about Guardian Books podcasts at theguardian.com/books

Guardian Books

10 following   View all

You can also add your own url or anchor text backlink from your audio description box.

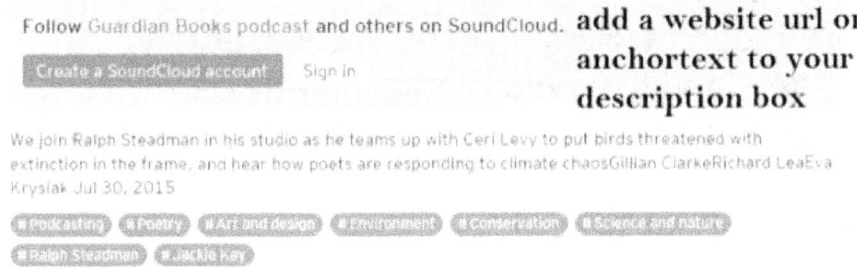

Follow Guardian Books podcast and others on SoundCloud.

add a website url or anchortext to your description box

Create a SoundCloud account   Sign in

We join Ralph Steadman in his studio as he teams up with Ceri Levy to put birds threatened with extinction in the frame, and hear how poets are responding to climate chaosGillian ClarkeRichard LeaEva Kryslak Jul 30, 2015

#Podcasting #Poetry #Art and design #Environment #Conservation #Science and nature #Ralph Steadman #Jackie Kay

With this method, you'll probably get a result in as little as 5 days.

How to structure your links

This is one of the most important SEO lessons you'll ever read. Make sure that you understand this before creating any backlinks. For you to understand this much better, I decided to do an example as if I'm backlinking to my own website.

Let's say I have a website about Texas bbq sauce.

Site name: www.Johny Blaze.com

Target keyword: TX BBQ Sauce

So I want to rank for the keyword TX BBQ Sauce

What I would do is create a page about it, put a 1,000 word article review.

The url of my new page would look like this.

www.JohnyBlaze.com/texas-bbq-sauce

HOWEVER, if your website is already TEXASBBQSAUCE.COM (exact match domain), I suggest that you change that new page's url to

TEXASBBQSAUCE.COM/TX-BARBEQUE

DO NOT REPEAT THE SAME WORD ON YOUR URL

This will trigger over optimization and will get your site penalize.

LINK STRUCTURE

When you build your backlinks, make sure that you'll use LSI keywords. These are keywords related to your main keyword but not exactly the same word.

In our example, www.JohnyBlaze.com/texas-bbq-sauce

Your main keyword is **texas bbq sauce**

When you build your backlinks, do not just use the exact keyword (texas bbq sauce) for every link that you'll create.

So for every 15 links that you'll create, only use your main keyword once or twice (max).

This is how your links schedule could be:

(the url is the backlink destination)

(the anchor text is the text you'll use to link to that url)

(http://, www. – they count as different backlink destination in the eyes of Google)

Anchor text	Backlink Destination URL

1st backlink – Texas Barbeque - http://johnyblaze.com

2nd backlink - Texas - http://johnyblaze.com

3rd backlink - JohnyBlaze - http://www.johnyblaze.com

4th backlink - http://johnyblaze.com - http://www.johnyblaze.com

5th backlink – www.johnyblaze.com - http://www.johnyblaze.com

6th backlink - click here - www.johnyblaze.com

7th backlink - **texas bbq sauce** - www.JohnyBlaze.com/texas-bbq-sauce

8th backlink - TX BBQ SAUCE - www.JohnyBlaze.com/texas-bbq-sauce

9th backlink - texas barbeque sauce - http://www.JohnyBlaze.com/texas-bbq-sauce

10th backlink – bbq sauce - Johnyblaze.com

11th backlink - City of Alamo - www.johnyblaze.com

12th backlink – Johny Blaze Home based factory - http://johnyblaze.com

13th backlink – TX's bbq hot sauce - www.JohnyBlaze.com/texas-bbq-sauce

14th backlink - San Antonio - http://johnyblaze.com

15th backlink – organic pigs - http://www.JohnyBlaze.com/

16th backlink – Blaze - http://Johnyblaze.com

And that's how you structure your links.

Notice how I only use the main keyword once, and the page url at only 4 times.

I did this to not get over optimized.

In addition, you'll spread the building of these links into a few days or week.

I suggest that you build 1 backlink every other day to be safe.

If you plan to build 16 high quality backlinks, you'll spread it from 15-30 days.

NOTE: IF YOU ARE BUILDING MASS BACKLINKS, FOLLOW THE SAME FORMULA.

ONLY 2-3% OF YOUR MASS BACKLINKS WILL BE FOR YOUR MAIN KEYWORD/S,

THE OTHER 97% OF YOUR BACKLINKS WILL BE LSI KEYWORDS.

Step 5 - Fulfilling the Order

The only thing we need is the buyers address that we will then send to our ALIEXPRESS or EBAY vendor.

Please take note that the process of fulfilling order that I'm gonna show you is via 1 customer per transaction only. Which means you have to repeat the process over and over again if you have a lot of orders. If you have a lot of orders coming, I suggest that you talk to your vendor and tell him that you will just send an excel file at the end of the day with the name and the address of your buyers, so you don't have to manually type the order on Aliexpress.

1 by 1 order fulfillment

This one is super easy.

You simply order like you would normally order on Aliexpress.

You need to register for a free account before you can order.

Choose your shipping method
And Click the BUY NOW button.

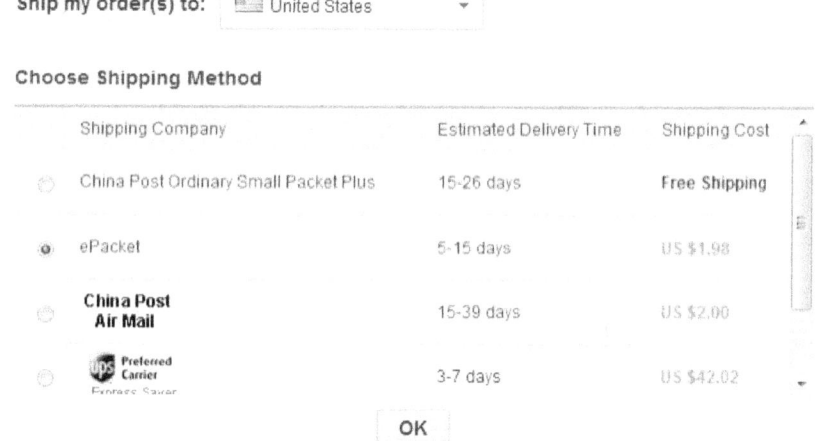

Shipping: **Free Shipping** to
United States via China Po
Estimated Delivery Time: 15-26

Quantity: 1 piece (487 pieces

Total Price: **US $1.01**

Buy Now

Now, instead of using your own address, you'll simply change the address and add a new one. Put your customers address, name and other information and place your order.

Once you confirm your order, your vendor will email you a confirmation and tracking for shipping. Send it to your customers and you're done!

Conclusion

So you finished this book, got the information you needed to succeed, I gave you all the things you need to start without capital – what's your remaining excuse?

Seriously, there should be none.

The only thing you should be doing right now is taking action, finding products to sell, creating a website and marketing your product.

Heck, you can do all of these steps in 1 or 2 days!

I laid out the process meticulously so you don't have to worry about not knowing what to do next or being stuck.

You only really have 2 options just like Neo from *The Matrix*.

1 – Take the Blue Pill, you stay where you are and wonder why your finances suck.

2 – Take the Red Pill, take chances, start something new, create a business and let it take you to a whole new level.